Siberian Husky Training:

The Ultimate Guide to Training Your Siberian Husky Puppy

Siberian Husky Training: The Ultimate Guide to Training Your Siberian Husky Puppy

Includes Sit, Stay, Heel, Come, Crate, Leash, Socialization, Potty Training and How to Eliminate Bad Habits

Brittany Boykin

Siberian Husky Training: The Ultimate Guide to Training Your Siberian Husky Puppy

Published by CAC Publishing LLC.

ISBN 978-1-950010-03-5 paperback

ISBN 978-1-950010-02-8 eBook

Table of Contents

Introduction

The Siberian Husky is easily one of the most widely accepted and recognized dog breeds anywhere in the world. This classically beautiful breed is known for its amazing versatility coupled with extreme intelligence. A Siberian Husky is capable of assuming many different roles, including:

- Companion dog

- Family pet

- Herding dog

- Show dog

- Obedience dog

- Working dog

- Guide dog for the blind

- Hearing dog for the deaf

- Search and rescue dog

- Tracking dog

- Hunting dog

- TV actors

... and many more

Siberian Huskies are characterized by their superior intelligence, high curiosity, boundless energy, versatility and regal good looks. These clever dogs can be very easy to train and can seem almost eager to learn new tricks and ways of pleasing their owners at very young ages.

However, as intelligent and easy to train as they may seem, there are times when some Siberian Husky owners may begin to feel frustrated and impatient when they don't see much success from their efforts. This can happen when your training methods don't take into consideration what's important to your dog and what makes him want to obey you the most.

Is a Siberian Husky Right for You?

As attractive a breed as the Siberian Husky might seem, it's important to remember they're not right for everyone. Due to their natural high intelligence and curiosity, these dogs need plenty of mental stimulation to keep them from becoming bored.

Siberian Huskies require plenty of exercise. Taking your dog out for walks regularly is important for more than just their physical health, your daily walk also provides him with some mental stimulation and some quality bonding time with his human.

This breed of dog is also capable of intense loyalty to his/her person, forming a life-long bond that is almost impossible to break. They'll love you unconditionally and want to do those things he thinks may please you most.

When a Siberian Husky forms a close bond with his human, he will think of a myriad of ways to try and get his human's attention – whether good or bad. This can mean pulling laundry from the line, digging holes or chewing your shoes if he believes that's the only way you'll focus your attention back on him again.

This kind of destructive behavior can become present in any breed of dog, but with a dog of high intelligence and a strong sense of family bonding, it's more important than ever to find ways to re-direct these instincts into more positive behaviors while your dog is still young.

Siberian Huskies crave companionship. To them, you and your family are his pack. They do not make good kennel dogs and won't respond well to being left alone in the backyard for long hours on end. This breed of dog is more likely to suffer from separation anxiety than some others if not taught early on how to deal with you leaving for work.

If you don't have the time or the patience to offer a Siberian Husky the training, exercise and companionship it craves, then perhaps consider looking into a different breed of dog.

Nothing is as enjoyable and exciting as getting a new companion animal. Dog lovers know that the unconditional love of a devoted dog is like no other – loyal, generous and constant.

Undoubtedly, you'll want to get off to a good start with your new companion, to establish and maintain that level of devotion. What's the best approach? Dog owners and trainers will tell you: the key to a great relationship with your dog is to be firm in your approach to problem behavior avoidance, and obedience, from day one.

If you find yourself admiring other owners and their dogs and wondering how they get their dog or puppy to sit, fetch and stay

– have heart. If you're willing to follow the guidelines in this book and give your dog and the training your time and effort, you'll find your dog will be as obedient and responsive as you could wish. It's best to start training when the dog is young – ideally, at just a few months old. At that age, a puppy is impressionable, open to learning, and longing to please. You'll have a great deal of influence, and that's important because the work you do with your dog now will determine the dog he or she will become. This time is an investment in having a great companion animal for years to come.

The chapters that follow will guide you in training your dog, using commands, repetition, and reward. For example, let's look at how you can train your dog to obey one of the most basic and important commands: "come."

No doubt you recognize the importance of teaching your dog to come when called. Your dog should be a companion to you, and that means he should obey when you call. In addition to obedience making your relationship stronger and more enjoyable, it's necessary for safety – if your dog is running full speed toward a busy street, or other source of danger, it's vital that he ignores his own wants and instincts and return to you if you call.

As with other commands you'll be teaching your dog, the

technique is simple, and it's repetition that will teach your dog to obey the command each and every time. Start by deciding what command you will use to tell your dog to come to you-you will use that one command, consistently. Prepare to teach the command by holding a toy in one of your hands, and a treat in the other. Now, walk away from your dog, holding the toy out and using the command to call the dog to you. Once he comes to you, give him the treat.

It's that simple! Now – do it again. And again. And perhaps one more time – then give your dog a long break from training, at least a couple of hours. Repeat the series of exercises two or three times more during the day, with a toy in one hand and a treat in the other. Give long breaks in between training sessions, so your dog doesn't get bored. In no time, you'll be pleased to find you've done it – your dog comes, consistently, when called.

Simple, right? And I think you'll find it's enjoyable, too, for both you and your dog. Basic dog training gives your dog confidence in himself, and confidence in you. It's fun, and it doesn't take long – just five minutes or so a few times a day, to begin, and then even shorter periods of time once your dog begins to get the hang of the command. Remember – it's important to reward both of you. Praise and treats for him – a pat on your back for you, for being patient and consistent.

This example gives you an idea of the simple, effective approach you'll find as you make your way through this book.

Our opening chapter looks at how to get off to a good start with a new puppy. Then we turn to training, taking a look at the other basic commands an obedient dog knows, and how to train your dog to obey them.

Chapter 1: Getting Off to a Good Start

Choosing a Siberian Husky Puppy

Siberian Husky puppies are cute, fluffy and so irresistible, it's easy to see why so many people choose these gorgeous pups as potential pets.

If you intend to show or breed your dog, then always choose a reputable breeder who is willing to give you the complete family lineage and registration papers. This can help you determine the most likely size, coat length, coloring and even temperament the litter is likely to display as dominant features.

With purebred Siberian Huskies, you should also ask about the medical histories of both the sire and the dam, as this breed can have hereditary medical and psychological issues to watch for.

These can include hip or joint dysplasia, arthritis, heart problems, higher risk of the potentially fatal 'canine bloat' (gastric dilatation or gastric digestive volvulus syndrome) and other serious genetic problems.

What most people forget is that these adorable puppies grow into large, powerful dogs very quickly, so you could be dealing with a 75-pound dog with the mind and behavior of a playful, mischievous puppy.

It's at this point that many unprepared owners give up on their dog. They'll give away the naughty pup or leave him at a shelter rather than taking the time to train them properly to become the loyal, loving, intelligent dog they all have the potential to be.

For the best results, you should begin basic training the moment your puppy comes home for the first time.

Siberian Husky puppies are incredibly smart. They'll pick up simple commands very quickly, and if you remember to interact with them in a language they understand, it's possible to show your puppy how to modify his own behavior to suit the family 'pack' rules even while he's still very young.

The key to training such intelligent breeds of dog is to have plenty of patience and learn to work with the praise and reward method. This is especially true with Siberian Huskies, who respond very well to praise.

Your dog will develop a strong sense of respect for you as you spend time working to teach him, train him and discipline him, to the point that he'll happily do as you command because he knows it pleases you, which pleases him in return.

You will also find that such high levels of intelligence can also come with equally high levels of stubbornness and the need to dominate. In dogs, domination isn't about aggression or violence. It's about trying to establish the pack order, and your puppy will work on lots of ways to try and figure out where his position is in your family pack.

Bringing Puppy Home

Bringing your puppy home for the first time can be an exciting day for you – but it's a stressful, scary day for your new puppy. After all, he's had the comfort and company of 6 or 7 litter-mates, plus his mother, since the day he was born. Now all he has is an unfamiliar new pack.

A puppy might seem like he's enjoying playtime immensely when he first arrives, but the moment he's left on his own, the sudden loneliness will remind him that his mother is missing and he has no litter-mates to cuddle up to for warmth and comfort.

This is where a conscientious owner will provide somewhere safe and reassuring for a new puppy to sleep and offer him a replacement litter-mate to help him feel safe. One of the easiest ways to do this is to buy or create a comfortable bed and give him an old stuffed toy that is a little larger than he is.

That old stuffed toy may start out as a replacement litter-mate in the beginning and end up being your puppy's friend and playmate as he grows up.

Puppy training also begins on that very first day home. This is when you establish ground rules for what's acceptable behavior and what's not. Potty training should also be a high priority right from the beginning.

While your pup might seem small and cute right now, he will grow into a large dog, so it's not wise to encourage him to jump, bite or get onto human furniture at any time. You should also never give your puppy anything of your own to play with or chew. Always provide him with his own toys and bedding and spend some time teaching him to seek out his own things rather than yours.

Always remember to curb any puppy behavior you wouldn't like to see in an adult dog. This way your Siberian Husky will grow up understanding what belongs to him and what belongs to you. He'll also have a healthy respect for the family-home rules very early on.

There's nothing as exciting and joyful as bringing a new puppy home. Puppies are full of life, trusting and spontaneous. It's no wonder pictures and videos of them are such a big draw on social media, and that everyone wants to hold, cuddle and play with these little balls of fur. It's all about the fun and the newness of the experience – it's likely thoughts of training are not uppermost in your mind when a new puppy comes into your life.

But for you and your puppy to have a strong and enjoyable relationship, it's important that your new companion's training begins as soon as possible. In many ways, a puppy is easier to train than an older dog. For one thing, you don't have to overcome periods of time in which the dog was badly trained, or untrained.

On the downside, a puppy is impulsive and full of energy. You'll probably find your puppy is more easily distracted than an older dog. For a puppy, every moment is another opportunity to find something new, get excited about it, and lose focus. So, in the beginning, you'll need to keep training sessions brief, and, to keep the puppy's enthusiasm, make sure each session ends on a positive note.

Speaking Your Dog's Language

A responsible Siberian Husky owner will always take time to learn how to communicate effectively with their dog. This means learning to speak in a language your dog will understand.

When you give a dog a command or talk to him, he doesn't listen to the words you say. Rather, he's responding to the tone of voice and the position of your body.

If you listen to your dog, you'll notice he has a range and variety of different barks, ranging from warning barks, happy barks, greeting yaps, growls, whines, whimpers, playful yips, attention seeking calls and excitable or playful barks. Each of these is tone-based and has a variety of lengths and meanings.

To encourage your dog to continue repeating an acceptable or pleasing behavior, praise him using a high-pitched, happy voice. You might even use an affectionate pat, or even a small food reward if you're especially happy with something he's done right, to reinforce that's he's done well and you're pleased.

However, if he's being bad or doing something unacceptable, giving a short reprimand that sounds a little like a low growl, such as 'ah ah,' will remind him of the little guttural growls his mother would make to scold him when he was naughty. He should stop doing whatever earned him that reprimand.

Yelling at a dog is never seen as scolding in dog language. Your dog will assume you're giving out the same warning barks that he is, or he will assume you're being aggressive at some threat he can't see or perceive. If you yell at a dog, you risk making him tense, but you won't be effectively disciplining him in any way. In fact, yelling at him could be making his bad behavior even worse.

A reassuring, loving tone of voice is fine for when your dog is having a goofy, affectionate moment with you, but giving this same reassurance during a time of stress or fear won't help your dog to feel better.

In fact, if you reassure a dog while he's feeling fear, such as through a thunderstorm, then he may interpret your kind words as being told he was right to be scared.

Offering your dog any kind of reward just for being cute gives him the impression that he doesn't have to obey your commands to get treats. After all, if he waits long enough, he knows you'll give him something to eat.

It's also wise to distinguish the difference between bribery and reward. Your dog should only receive treats after he's done something to earn them. He shouldn't have to be shown a reward or bribed into behaving by waving a treat in front of his nose.

Always consider how your dog hears your tone of voice when you're working on training techniques, when you're scolding him, or when you're playing. Remember that treats are to be earned and you'll soon find your dog will understand what's expected of him much more easily.

Socializing Your Puppy

Equally important as training is your puppy's socialization. Socialization is vital to reaching the kind of relationship you want with your dog and setting clear expectations. It's important that socialization begin as early as possible, as a very young puppy is far more open to being socialized than an older dog, or even an older puppy. Sad to say, a puppy that isn't properly socialized by the age of four months may never be able to develop the socialization he needs to enjoy life with others or be enjoyed by others.

Socialization doesn't just make the puppy more enjoyable and happier – it also makes him safer. It keeps him from growing too aggressive with people and with other dogs. It's especially important that he learn how to be in a social situation with other dogs, as aggression with other dogs could lead to fights and harm to him and others.

Socialization takes place naturally in the litter, with the puppy playing with siblings. As they play with each other, they try new things – and learn what kind of behavior is appropriate, and gets a good response, and what type of behavior is disapproved of, and results in a negative response. For example, if the puppy bites too hard he may find his siblings return that rough behavior or they or his mother may express disapproval in other ways. As time goes on, the puppy learns appropriate behavior through trial and error.

It's unfortunate that, these days, socialization is hampered because puppies are removed from their mothers too soon, to be sold or adopted. You can offset this by providing puppy play sessions. You'll find that any good puppy training programs provide free and open time for puppies to interact.

As your puppy's owner, it's your responsibility to introduce him to a wider range of experiences and places. You aren't just training him to function in your home, behind closed doors; a good companion animal can handle a number of situations in a way that's obedient and responsive.

Why You Should Socialize Your Puppy

Proper socialization teaches your puppy not to fear other dogs. It also helps them work off all that excess puppy energy!

When your puppy socializes with other dogs of any age, they learn lessons that help them become better companion animals to you and your family. Studies show that dogs that were less socialized as puppies are likely to be more destructive, harder to train, less obedient, more hyperactive, and in general, have more problem behaviors than other dogs.

In particular, insufficient socialization often causes puppies to behave in fearful and aggressive ways. Aggressive dogs are generally afraid. For a dog to develop into a good companion animal to you and your family, he should be socialized not to just other dogs, but to people, especially children. To understand why, consider that dogs see humans very differently; they make a clear distinction between the owner they see as their pack leader and other adults, and they make a clear distinction between adults and children. To learn appropriate behaviors, it's important for puppies to be socialized with a variety of adults, children, and other dogs of various ages.

As with other training, it's best to address your puppy's socialization with young children when young – ideally, before your dog is four months old. For one thing, it's safer for the child if your puppy is smaller when its socialization takes place.

How to Socialize

A good outing to try is going to a pet store that is accepting and friendly to having its canine customers along for the shopping. More and more, pet stores are allowing owners and families to bring their dog along. As you can imagine, the sights and smells in a pet store give your puppy a lot of opportunities to respond and interact. Just make sure the store you go to is open to having you bring your puppy along.

If your puppy was removed from its mother and siblings too early, take responsibility for giving your puppy the experiences he should have gotten from littermates. For example, there are acceptable ways for a puppy to bite and unacceptable ways. Puppies naturally bite when they play and wrestle. They have thick skin that protects them, but sometimes they bite too hard. Then, the mother will reprimand the puppy by holding him by the scruff of the neck until he submits. The lesson is clear – biting is natural in playing, but biting too hard gets reprimanded.

So give your puppy a chance to play with other puppies, or with gentle, friendly, socialized adult dogs. Many adult dogs have a natural nurturing instinct and will help the puppy learn what's appropriate in the same way its mother would have. Seek out puppy play dates or kindergarten classes. And try not to hover too much when your puppy interacts with others; let the puppies play on their own and work out any issues that arise, even if it leads to some roughness and squealing. Certainly, protect your puppy, but realize a certain amount of negative experience is all part of the learning process.

You'll notice the order of hierarchy becomes apparent during the socialization process. Some puppies respond by being submissive, and you'll see them roll over and bare their throats at the first sign of aggression. Of course, other puppies take a more dominant role, making their will known and trying to force other puppies to do what they want. Watch your puppy during these interactions. The way he responds will give you valuable insight into how to approach your relationship with him, and the training you do with him.

Socialization includes humans as well as other dogs. You can help your puppy interact with people in all kinds of ways – at the classes you go to with him, and, when appropriate, in day to day life. Be sure you give your puppy a diverse sampling of people – old and young, male and female, black and white. His perception of each may be different; help him learn he can successfully and safely interact with the people he'll meet throughout his life.

And don't limit his interaction with other animals to just other dogs, particularly if you have other animals in your household.

Let him get to know friendly cats, willing rabbits, curious guinea pigs and more. Just be sure you are watchful and ensure that both animals are safe. Start by introducing the puppy to the smell – and just the smell – of the other animal. Use its bedding, or a toy it plays with frequently. After a few exposures to the smell, your puppy is much more likely to accept the animal itself.

Teaching Your Puppy Proper Socialization Skills

Socialization matters - a well-socialized dog is a happy dog and one that other people and animals enjoy being around. On the other hand, a dog that hasn't been properly socialized is a danger to you, himself and others. It's your responsibility to give your dog proper socialization and to make wise choices depending on his ability to handle social situations.

Remember that the lessons a puppy learns in socialization – good or bad – are hard to undo. Those experiences will affect him the rest of his life. Socialize well and wisely.

What does proper socialization provide? Ideally, a dog was thoroughly and properly socialized with its litter and its mother at a very young age. As a result, he is at ease with other dogs, other animals and people, neither frightened and submissive, nor overly aggressive. He is confident, even in unfamiliar places and situations.

A dog that hasn't been properly socialized is much more likely to bite from fear. As such, he is a liability to you, and a danger to you, himself and others. He is much less able to adapt to a new location or a new situation. Without proper socialization, something as simple and necessary as a visit from friends, or a trip to the veterinarian, can cause stress and reactions that are both unpleasant and dangerous.

What to do if your puppy wasn't properly socialized? If your puppy didn't stay with his mother and siblings up to the age of 12 weeks, do your best to give him the same kind of exposure and experience he should have had. And continue to socialize, even after your puppy is three months old.

There are so many definite do's and don'ts when it comes to properly socializing any puppy.

Socialization Do's

- It's important to make socialization fun for your puppy, and never let them become threatening. In particular, ensure your puppy's first socialization experience is a positive one; if you don't, it will set his progress back several weeks at the least, and could hold him back from being properly socialized for the rest of his life.

- Make play dates at your house or apartment, letting your

puppy play with other dogs that are friendly and healthy, in an environment in which he feels safe. When he has a few positive play dates with other dogs, introduce other animals and pets, such as hamsters, rabbits, and, in particular, flexible and friendly cats. With any and all animals you introduce to your puppy, make sure vaccinations – his and theirs – are up to date.

- Make play dates with people as well, by inviting your friends and family over to engage in and play with the new puppy. Include several people, of diverse backgrounds – men and women, children and adults, old people and young, and people from diverse ethnic backgrounds.

- At the beginning of his socialization, let your puppy be socialized in surroundings he knows and feels safe in. As socialization progresses, take the puppy to a variety of places to meet people and other animals. Include pet stores, parks, school playgrounds, or just stop to speak to people as you walk your puppy around the neighborhood. When you feel socialization is going well, introduce him to public events where there are crowds, noise, and lots of activity. He needs to be able to function well in any situation you place him in, as long as you know he's safe.

- Some dogs dislike riding in the car, so socialize your puppy to car rides as well. Make them pleasant – stop from time to time to let the puppy for a walk outside the car. If he's uneasy in the car, take along a special treat that he only gets when he rides in the car, so he'll associate it with something positive and appealing.

- You may have found yourself smiling at dogs that showed an irrational fear of inanimate objects – brooms, vacuum cleaners, newspapers or umbrellas. But it's important that your dog is calm and confident in any situation, so expose your puppy to all kinds of objects that you think might frighten him. Allow him to explore such items on his own, in a safe environment, so he can learn he needn't fear them.

- Train your puppy to adapt by moving his toys from one area to another, or rearranging the furniture. He'll learn to adapt and be confident that he can adapt to change.

- De-sensitize your puppy to the things he'll experience at the vet or the groomer's, such as being brushed, having nails trimmed, ears touched and cleaned, mouth opened, and paws examined. It's natural for a dog to resist some of these things, but helping your puppy get used to them will make routine visits much more pleasant for all.

- Introduce the puppy to things around the house that make noise or present challenges – the doorbell, stairs, the vacuum, the smoke alarm. Let him see these things are common, and nothing bad happens when he has to experience or hear them.

Socialization Don'ts

There are likewise things you will want to avoid when socializing a puppy:

- Do not let your puppy interact with animals you don't know; in particular, don't set him down when a strange animal is nearby. Any interaction, and particularly an attack, could traumatize your dog and delay his progress.

- Be aware that your instinct to protect and comfort your puppy could inadvertently reinforce his fears. When your puppy shows fear of any kind, your instinct may be to offer support and soothe him; but doing so could actually reinforce his fear. Instead, calmly adjust the situation, removing the source of his fear, or, if it's appropriate, help him become desensitized to it. Be aware that if your dog unexpectedly shows signs of biting, it could well be evidence that he's afraid.

- Socialization should be fun for you and your puppy, so take your time and enjoy it. Offer him several opportunities over a span of several weeks, and be patient – allow the puppy to progress in his own time, and at his own pace.

- Arrange for the socialization to be short, especially in the beginning. Young puppies, like young children, have short attention spans; the socialization should only last as long as he and you are engaged and enjoying it.

- Remember that it's important to begin socialization as early in your puppy's life as you can. A young puppy is trusting, curious and impressionable – take advantage of the time when he has these qualities, and give him as many positive socialization opportunities as possible, so he'll develop strong socialization skills.

Supporting Good Behavior, Discouraging Bad

As with any dog, your puppy will respond best to love, time spent with him, patience, and praise. Do your best to structure the training and environment to give plenty of opportunities to praise your dog. The praise of your puppy will have much more impact if you get down to eye level with him. Eye-level praise, attention, and affection go a long way toward reinforcing the lesson.

Likewise – be sure not to reward him for behavior you object to. You may have to go against your instinct. For example, if your puppy jumps on someone, it may be tempting to laugh because he's small, and it's cute. But one day he'll weigh three times as much, and it won't be cute anymore. Lay groundwork now by setting good boundaries and enforcing them.

- A good way to handle unwanted behavior is to redirect — for example, if your puppy is jumping on someone, direct him to sit, and praise and reward him when he does.

- Rely on positive reinforcement and praise to potty train, too, rather than shaming and anger. Praise his successes. Be realistic about accidents — he's essentially a baby, and he's developing muscle control and working to understand expectations.

Setting the Stage for Success

- Do your best to control the environment the first time your puppy comes home and meets the family. Have all family present, and choose a time that is calm so you can give your time and attention to his debut. Holidays are probably the worst time to introduce a new puppy to his new home. There's way too much activity, excitement, and distractions. Choose to introduce your puppy to the family and the home at a better time.

- Help your puppy acclimate to your home. If there are stairs, help him slowly become familiar with them. Puppies are often afraid of stairs; let him take his time and help him build his confidence slowly. A good way to begin is to start at the bottom of the stairs, rather than the top, and urge the puppy to climb a step or two. If he bounds up the stairs, great! If he shows signs of stress, let one or two steps do for this introduction. Go up on the first step yourself; then urge the puppy to join you, using a treat or toy. Then go down, invite him to join you there, and reward again. Be patient; this is a time when it's best to take one step at a time, literally.

- It's important your puppy learn to be comfortable wearing a collar, so take time to purchase the right collar to ensure he'll accept it. A collar that is chosen for your puppy's size, and fits properly, is less likely to cause fear and his frantic attempts to pull the collar off. Your basic collar should be a sturdy collar of a soft material and should fasten by buckling. Specialty collars, such as choke and training collars are useful, but they should only be used when needed for a particular type of training. Your puppy's ID tag and license should be attached to the collar, so if you and your puppy become separated, he's wearing the information needed to return him to you.

- Collars sometimes cause puppies fear. Be prepared for the possibility your puppy will not like the collar, and let him claw at it, squirm, roll over and rub against things with it. Don't try to soothe him; neither should you reprimand him. Just let him make his peace with it on his own. After a minute or two, you might introduce a distraction, such as a treat or toy. Once your puppy has some experiences while wearing the collar, he'll get used to it and won't react to it at all.

Chapter 2: How Much is Enough Exercise

It's always sad to hear people say 'My dog doesn't need that much exercise. He seems happy to lie around at my feet all day.' This is never a good reason to assume your dog doesn't need the mental and physical exercise – especially with a working breed like the Siberian Husky.

It's true that many Siberian Huskies seem at their happiest when they're allowed to curl up anywhere near their owner and will stay there for hours on end. In fact, I have a Siberian Husky curled up under my desk at my feet while I write at this very moment.

This is predominantly because a Siberian Husky will feel happy to be included in whatever you're doing, but it isn't enough for his physical health and well-being.

Walking

Your dog won't view being taken out for a walk as 'exercise time.' He views it as being invited out by the family pack for a 'hunt.' He knows he'll have the opportunity to look around for potential food, sniff around for other dogs or potential prey, and spend some quality time as part of the pack as well. For him, this constitutes mental stimulation as well.

Siberian Huskies will naturally travel in a cantering-lope rather than a slow walk. During your walks together, be sure you move at a brisk pace so your dog can trot alongside you in a comfortable gait for his size. This can mean walking quickly or even jogging to make sure you keep at the speed of his gait without him needing to pull ahead.

Walking is also great for keeping knee, hip and elbow joints supple in this large breed of dog. Large breeds, like Siberian Huskies, are known to suffer from hip problems later in life, so regular exercise can help to keep your beloved dog fit and healthy for much longer.

Play-Time

Siberian Huskies are naturally playful, inquisitive and curious. A bored dog can quickly become destructive as he looks for things to occupy his mind. This can mean digging holes in your garden, ripping laundry off the line, chewing your favorite shoes or barking out of sheer boredom.

Play-time is about giving him a bit of time to be a bit silly and have some fun, but it's also an important time to reinforce the bond between you and your dog.

Play-time should be an important part of your dog's exercise routine and should be something your dog finds fun and entertaining. This can mean teaching your dog to fetch a ball or Frisbee and then throwing it around for him in the yard or at the park. Most Siberian Huskies love to play a game of tug-of-war, so find a suitable rope-toy and encourage him to play with you. This helps to strengthen shoulder and jaw muscles.

You can also incorporate games that stimulate his mind and his need to hunt, such as hide-and-seek. Siberian Huskies enjoy tracking down an owner who is hiding in a closet, behind a bush, around the side of the house or behind a door, so make it a fun game and praise him when he finds you.

Hunting

While Siberian Huskies love to spend some time hunting and tracking down potential prey, this does NOT mean you need to take your dog out to kill wild animals. It can mean giving him something in his own yard to track and hunt that is rewarding for him mentally and physically.

It's possible to give them a small taste of the 'hunt' when they're out on their daily walk, but try scattering a handful of kibble or biscuits across your yard and telling him to go and find them. He'll spend as long as it takes sniffing every one of them out.

Many dog owners use specifically made, non-toxic chew toys designed to hold kibble inside. Your dog will happily spend time trying to work out how to get the food out. Don't use sticky or wet food, or you may find you attract ants rather than entertaining your dog.

These simple games can help your dog learn to hunt down food rewards and track any hidden treats you might leave around.

Chapter 3: The Basics of Dog Obedience Training

Obedience training is a must if you want your relationship with your dog to be everything it can be. People do obedience training for exactly that – obedience. But good training does so much more. It makes you happy because you have a companion dog you can rely on to obey and behave – that makes it so much easier to have a positive relationship, in any situation. It makes your dog happy because a properly trained puppy or dog is confident, happy and productive.

As you and your dog work on the training together, you build a strong relationship that confirms, with every command, that you are the leader of this pack, and that's a good thing for both you and your dog. Finally, the obedience angle is, indeed, important, as it makes your dog a valued and beloved member of the family, instead of an untrained dog that is nervous, neurotic, and possibly destructive or even dangerous.

Obedience training gives your dog something he very much needs – a leader (you) that he can follow. His background, clear back to the time when he was a member of a wolf pack, means he is hard-wired to want a leader he can follow. Without that leadership, the dog may take on the dominant role, himself, and that is unhealthy for him, for you, and your family. Just the time you spend with your dog in obedience training does a great deal to let him know that, in this relationship, you are the leader. Moreover, most dogs want to please their leader – their owner – and training gives your dog a clear understanding of what your expectations are, and how to please you.

The training essentially establishes for you and your dog the hierarchy of the wolf pack. Again and again, as your dog works with and follows your commands, he will be turning away from his own desires and impulses to obey what you ask of him. It's the same submissive response he would be giving to the leader in his pack of dogs or wolves.

Working together, you learn to communicate with each other. While this book covers a number of approaches to training, each is based on positive reinforcement, an approach in which you win your dog over so that he willingly cooperates with what you want him to do and be. Going into this training, there's one over-riding fact that is important for you to know: your animal's respect cannot and will not be won through force, rough handling, or punishment. It can only be earned through time spent together in a positive environment, in which you, as leader, train with techniques based on praise and mutual respect.

At its simplest, obedience training teaches your dog what you want him to do, and what you don't want him to do. It relies on a few basic commands that are covered in Chapter 3, that represent what you do want the dog to do. And the training also encompasses the things you don't want the dog to do, such as surging ahead when you walk with him, chewing your shoes and furniture, jumping on people, and generally being out of control.

And training is fun – or it should be – for both of you. It's a real joy when your dog realizes you are about to work together on further training, and his response is a positive one. Training is an important gift you are giving yourself, your family and your dog – it will make life more fulfilling, easier, and safer, in so many ways. It opens the world to your dog – you can safely take him on walks, to the beach, or the dog park.

You may be reading this book because you want to begin training with a new puppy, or you may be training an adult or older dog. Whatever the age of your dog, he can be trained successfully to obey commands and be an enjoyable companion. It is true that it's easier to train younger dogs – they won't have to un-learn bad habits or bad training first. But know that even a dog with behavior and confidence problems can be retrained successfully with the approaches found in this book.

The training of an adult dog is not the same as that of a younger dog. The younger the dog is, the shorter is his attention span. The younger your dog is, the shorter your training sessions will need to be to keep the training engaging and positive for your puppy or very young dog. Balanced with training is socialization – you should be taking time to socialize your puppy, as well as training him, as was covered in Chapter 1.

You may want to seek out obedience training classes for support and structure in training your dog. For puppies, especially, kindergarten and puppy training classes give structure and provide an opportunity for socialization as well.

Effective Discipline

Far too many people assume that to discipline a dog, they need to smack his nose or yell at him or tie him up alone in the yard or rub his nose in the mess he made. The truth is, none of these tactics work as effective discipline for any breed of dog. In fact, you could be making his behavior even worse.

To administer effective forms of discipline, it's important to understand a little bit about dog-language and then modify your disciplinary measures to suit something your dog will understand. Keep in mind that a dog is happiest when he can make his pack-leader happy. Hopefully, he views you as his pack-leader.

Never hit any dog, for any reason. In dog language, this is seen as unprovoked aggression. He doesn't understand why you're lashing out and could develop an unhealthy sense of fear of you. That fear could quickly turn into depression, anxiety, aggression or other psychological issues as your dog tries to figure out why you're violent toward him when all he wanted to do was play with you.

Always remember, an adult Siberian Husky has teeth and powerful jaws that could easily crush every bone in your hand. He just chooses not to. As a dog, he usually has unconditional love for his owner, regardless of how he's being treated.

If you've learned how to convey your pleasure with good actions, then you should already realize that your dog craves your approval, your attention, and your affection. In order to show him that you're not pleased with something, simply ignore him for a few minutes. Turn your back on him, fold your arms across your chest and look away. In dog language, this is a severe reprimand.

When he modifies his own behavior and is doing the right thing, lavishly praise on him with a happy, high-pitched tone of voice. Give him an affectionate pat as you say 'good dog.' He'll quickly learn that you're happy when he behaves well and he receives none of the things he wants most when he's acting badly.

It's also possible to modify bad behavior into good behavior fairly easily. For example, if you catch your dog chewing something of yours, remove the offending item and give him a short 'ah ah' and then replace it with one of his own toys. Praise him for playing with his own toy and he'll soon get the idea.

The Importance of Rewards

Rewards are an acknowledgment of good behavior and responsiveness. They make the training positive and give your dog a clear indication that his behavior is what you wanted and expected. Reward training is acknowledged by almost all trainers and handlers as the most enjoyable and effective method by which to train your dog, at the same time that you build a strong relationship with him.

Rewards and positive reinforcement make your dog eager and happy to participate in his training, so make it fun! Make it a game, so you can keep both you and your dog motivated to make the time for training, continually taking your training to the next step. Use treats the dog really enjoys. Bookend the training with play time, so you can make sure it always begins and ends on a positive note.

How This Book Approaches Training

Let's look at an example of how this book approaches training by showing how you might train your dog for the basic task of heeling, or walking with you on a loose lead. Often, this is the first command that is taught, and it's a good one to start with because dogs respond to it well with reward training.

Your first step is to purchase a good training lead and a training collar that fits your dog. Your local pet store or a professional trainer should be able to advise you on purchasing the correct collar.

Begin by walking with your dog, and notice his position. His head should be relatively even with your knee. That gives him the opportunity to anticipate how fast you're walking and when you're going to stop, or if you're going to turn. The whole purpose of training your dog to heel is for him to match your pace and your direction – not for you to ever match his.

As you're walking, if your dog surges ahead, gently pull on the leash. Pulling will engage the collar, and give your dog a reminder to slow down and match your pace. Give only as much of a tug as is needed to convey slow down, but if you need to give a stronger tug to make your dog obey, do so.

If your dog, instead, begins to fall behind you, slow down and gently urge him forward; he's learning what your wants and expectations are. You can use a toy or favorite piece of food to urge him forward until he's walking in the correct position at your side, his head relatively even with your knee. Once he's in the right position, keep the food or toy level with that position, to keep him in it.

You are waiting for the dog to understand that you want him to walk with his head by your knee, and to respond to your choices.

Speed up – he should speed up too. Slow down – turn. When he accommodates the change with his head remaining in the proper position, praise him enthusiastically, and give him a treat. Always remember: he will learn and do well through your positive reinforcement.

In the early days of training, it's best to reward for every good behavior with a bit of food and a lot of enthusiastic praise. Even your dog's slightest attempts to please should be rewarded. As training proceeds, you can scale back on the treats and reward your dog four times out of five with praise alone. That's really better for his nutrition and his waistline, as you don't want him always filling up on treats.

No matter what you may have been told by someone else, know that training based on punishment and scolding is not as effective as training that relies on positive reinforcement. Moreover, training based on negativity demoralizes your dog, hurts his confidence, and hurts his relationship with you. Sure, reprimands may be needed from time to time for such behaviors as jumping, chasing or biting; but at heart, most dogs very much want to please their owners – the leader of their pack. Reprimand to call your dog away from immediate danger, and then turn back to positive training again.

Here's an example. You come home after a long day, step

through the door, and see your dog chewing on your shoe. Watch your energy – don't overreact. Simply say "No!" or "Off!" (depending on what command you choose and will be using consistently), and take the shoe away from him, immediately handing him one of his toys instead. When he starts to chew on it, praise him enthusiastically, getting on eye-level with him if possible. You've just taught him what you expect – you expect him to chew, chewing his toy is good, chewing your shoe is not.

So take the time to teach your dog, whether puppy, adult or older dog, the behaviors you want. Train regularly, for short periods of time. Keep it positive and make it fun. You are investing in years of a wonderful relationship with your companion animal.

Chapter 4: The Six Basic Commands

You probably have a number of good reasons for wanting your dog to be calm, obedient and responsive to commands. If you're like most people, you're probably training your dog so it will be a better companion for you and your family.

It makes perfect sense to train your dog for your own reasons and your own enjoyment, but you should know that the training that follows also leads to a happier dog. And a safer one – your dog will be far less likely to have confrontations with other dogs and with people. Your friends and neighbors will very much appreciate that your dog is not a threat. As you might expect, studies have shown that thoroughly trained dogs are much less likely to attack, bite, or exhibit other behavioral problems.

If you're like most people, you're training your dog so it will be a better companion for you and your family.

And of course, training your dog well will also make him or her a much better family companion, especially in households where there are young children. Many studies have shown that proper dog training makes a big impact when it comes to cutting down the number of dog bites and other behavior problems encountered by dog owning households.

What makes a dog truly and thoroughly trained? Let's start with the basic commands every trained dog should be able to understand and follow. You may have another word for these commands, but the basic things a dog should know how to do are:

Come – for the sake of convenience and the safety of your dog and others, your dog should respond immediately when you call it to come to you.

Sit – the sit command puts your dog in a position of attentive waiting, better able to listen and pay attention to what you ask of it next.

Stay – you should be able to expect your dog to remain in place when you command him to.

Down – the down position establishes you as the "leader" of your dog's pack and gives you the authority needed to ensure your dog obeys more complex commands.

Heel – a good companion dog walks beside you on a loose lead, choosing his movements based on where he senses you are going, and never pulling on the lead or lagging behind you

Stopping – immediately – when he hears the word "No" – a well-trained dog immediately stops whatever he is doing when he hears you say the word "no." However, many scenarios you can imagine in which response to the "no" command would be essential – there are scores more. It's essential your dog knows and obeys this command.

Consistent obedience when he hears you give these six basic commands will give your dog a strong grounding for the more complex training that will follow. They will also go a long way toward correcting basic behavioral problems. Finally, they form the basis for more complex training that will follow, so it's important to fully master them before moving on.

In teaching these commands, it's best to teach them in this order, fully mastering one before moving on to the next. Remember – be patient, be consistent, and offer praise.

Teaching the Six Basic Commands

Sit

The Sit command is a good place to start your training. Initially, start your training in an area that's familiar to your dog, and free of distraction. Once your dog has the basic command mastered, you can move him to a more challenging area that's less familiar, and combine this command with the heel command.

To start, with your dog standing directly in front of you, have a small, tasty treat in your hand. Now simply put your hand – the one with the treat – a few inches from your dog's nose and move your hand up and over the back of his head, keeping your hand just a few inches away. Your dog will follow the treat with his head, and his tail end will end up on the ground in a sit. As soon as his behind makes contact with the ground, give him the treat and praise him.

Repeat this step a few times. Then, add the command. Just before you begin to move your hand, say "sit." Immediately move your hand as before, and give your dog lavish praise (and the treat) as soon as his back quarters make contact with the ground. Soon, your dog will be trained to respond to this command without the treat.

Once your dog has mastered "sit" in a familiar area, try it in more challenging areas, such as in your front yard or at a park. It's important that your dog knows to respond to the "sit" command at all times and in any place. Once mastered, you can combine the "sit" command with your work in teaching your dog the next command – to heel.

Heel

If you want to enjoy walking with your dog on a leash, training in how to heel is essential. It's pathetic to watch a dog owner dragged down the street by a large dog that's ignoring its owner's pleas to stop, slow down, behave. It's equally unpleasant to see owners having to drag a reluctant dog that's trying to lag behind. A well-behaved, well-trained dog will walk at your side, with its head generally in line with your knee – ready to respond when he senses you are slowing down, speeding up or turning.

In training to heel, use a training collar, and remember the dog's nose should generally be in line with your knee. When you begin to walk with your dog on the leash, if he gets ahead of you, gently tug on the leash. When you do, the training collar will tighten and gently remind the dog to fall back, keeping his nose in line with your knee.

If your dog falls behind you, gently urge him forward. You might try holding out a toy to lure him.

In the early stages of training, keep a steady pace. Once your dog has begun to master the heel and is walking at your side, his nose in line with your knee, try varying the pace so he can practice aligning his pace with yours. Remember: never adjust your pace to match the pace of your dog. It's his job to match your pace.

You can further this training by combining the "sit" command, and by challenging your dog to follow properly when you turn and go in other directions. These approaches will teach your dog to always watch for where you want to go, anticipate your movements, and accompany you smoothly and easily. Good dog!

To combine the heel training with "sit," as you are walking with your dog, stop abruptly. If your dog doesn't stop when you stop, just give a slightly sharp tug on the leash to remind your dog.

Once the dog has stopped by your side, give the "sit" command and urge him to sit by placing your hand on his hindquarters and pushing gently. Remember – don't use too much pressure, and push steadily and slowly, rather than abruptly.

As with all the training, repeat, repeat, repeat, with consistency and patience, until your dog responds as you want. You'll know your training is having the desired effect when you stop and your dog sits on his own, automatically, without the command.

Giving the "No" Command

It's imperative your dog know and respond to the word "no" promptly. This command will help avoid confusion about what behaviors you want, and what behaviors you don't.

"No" helps you tell your dog that he isn't doing what you want – it identifies unwanted behavior. Timing is important – say "no" clearly and a bit sharply immediately when your dog does something you don't want. Then follow with an action, such as removing the treat or pulling a bit on the leash. Note: your instinct may be to perform the action, then say "no." Reversing that – saying "no," and then performing the action – will get a better response and train your dog to respond to "no" more quickly.

The "Stay" Command

The "stay" command is another command that will lay the groundwork for more complex, advanced training, so it's important your dog masters this command.

Choose a time when your dog is relaxed and not too energetic (a walk before you teach this command may give your dog a good attitude toward the training).

You should have already mastered the "sit" command. Place your dog in a sit, and slowly begin to back away from him, holding the leash loosely. Your dog wants to be with you, and his instinct will probably be to stand and begin to follow you. When he does, return to him and again ask him to sit – then again, begin to back away.

As you repeat this process, your dog will begin to understand and will stay seated as you back away. Once your dog has mastered this step, you can move on to dropping the leash as you back away. Then drop it, and back further away. It's natural for your dog to become distracted, stand and begin to move. As always in this training, just remain patient, consistent, and lavish with praise when your dog performs well. He'll get there. It's a great feeling when you can put your dog in a "stay," move far away, and know he'll stay put. When that happens, lavish the praise, and give yourself a pat on the back, too.

The "Down" command

Teaching your dog the "down" command gives you the ability to keep him in one place. This command may take a bit longer, and a bit more patience, to teach, but it is useful helping your dog calm down when stressed and putting him in a position that will let others feel comfortable meeting and petting him.

Start with a treat in your hand, and your dog sitting or standing. Bend, let your dog briefly smell the treat, and begin to lower the treat to the floor. Say "down" as your dog begins to lower himself to the floor. Once he's all the way on the floor, you should have the treat between his paws. Give it to him – but only after he's all the way down on the floor. Then give praise.

Once your dog has mastered "down," combine it with "stay" to give you the ability to put your dog in a down position and know he will stay there.

One note: be sensitive to the surface your dog is on. Don't ask him to do "down" and "stay" on a hot or gravelly surface.

The "Off" command

The "off' command is a lesser-known command that is useful in training a dog not to chase cars, bikes, people or cats.

Bicycle riders will tell you how annoying – and frightening – it is when a dog chases them. And, your dog's instinct may be to chase – but that's what training is for. If your dog responds when he sees a bicyclist, cat, or other moving object, and begins to strain at the leash, simply say "off" and tug at the leash. With time and patience – and lavish praise for good behavior – your dog will learn to respond to the command, without the accompanying tug on the leash.

If you've completed this training and you and your dog have mastered these six commands, congratulations! You've made a great start in having a dog that's a loving and pleasant companion. But even more, you've done a great deal to strengthen the bond you have with your dog and reinforce your position as the pack leader. It may surprise you to know that a dog trained in obedience is a happier, more stable dog. Dogs are pack animals, and training supports your dog's need to know who the pack leader is, and trust them. So establishing yourself as pack leader means your dog will respond to your commands – and feel safe and secure in knowing he knows what's expected of him.

And consider the other advantages of this training. Your dog got exercise (good for him and you too, most likely!). He feels accomplished and more confident because you asked many things of him and he was able to comply. Essentially, you've given him work to do – as he's been bred to do for hundreds of years. Dogs were bred to herd, guard and protect. More often today, your dog is not a working animal so much as a companion animal – but the instinct and need to do work is still present for him, and this training helped satisfy that. You've given him something to do, and that goes a long way toward offsetting bad or neurotic behavior.

This training and the training you'll continue to do as you make your way through this book will engage his mind and body. That's an especially important accomplishment for high-energy breeds, like Siberian Huskies. All dogs, but high energy dogs in particular, need a place to put their extra energy, in a way that also brings them – and you - enjoyment.

The next chapters will look at various approaches to dog training, and help you choose the approach that's right for you and your dog.

Chapter 5: Training with a Leash or Collar

You probably know there are a wide variety of approaches to dog training. How do you choose the one that's right for you? The following chapters describe the intent and approaches of various forms of training. All meet the primary guideline: that they build a strong, positive and trusting relationship between the owner and the dog, based on getting and keeping the dog's respect (which shouldn't be hard to do, as it's in the nature of dogs to want a leader, and to follow their chosen leader's direction).

The most traditional approaches to training are leash training and collar training. Both have a long history of proven success. At the same time, dogs vary, and individual personalities vary as well. As you read these approaches to training, you'll likely spot the one that best fits your dog, and you.

Personalities within Siberian Huskies can vary, and the experiences your dog has had, both before he came to you and since, are an influence. Read about these approaches to training, choose one that you think fits you and the dog best, and, if you are seeking a trainer, seek a trainer that offers that approach to training.

For many owners, the traditional approach of leash or collar training will be appropriate and produce the results they want. These two approaches are particularly useful if you will need to train your dog to be particularly reliable – if he will have a job to do such as rescue work, or serving as a guard dog or police dog.

These two types of training use force in varying degrees – from a slight prompt given with the lead, to more harsh corrections. For the training to be effective, it's important that the degree of force used is appropriate to each training situation.

Collar - and leash-based training first teaches the dog the behavior – generally, using the leash. Once the dog shows understanding of and obedience to the command, the lead is henceforth used to correct the dog if he doesn't obey as needed. In collar and leash training, the trainer uses the leash to control and communicate with the dog.

With this type of training, it's important that the dog trusts the trainer, and will obey without question. The test of whether or not the dog is fully and successfully trained is the trainer's ability to put the dog into a posture or position the dog is resisting – one the dog does not want to take. While that doesn't mean using force, it usually requires some level of manipulation, and that manipulation is done using the leash, for reasons of safety and ease.

So the leash functions as a training tool, and during training, an important tool. Once training ends, the goal is for the trainer to obtain obedience without the leash, or using another tool.

An example of another kind of tool would be the owner's body, signals, and skill. Using those, the handler would need to be able to expect obedience. For that reason, it's important to create a relationship in which the trainer is clearly the leader, and the dog is clearly the follower. The leash should not be used as a crutch, and a dog that's been properly trained should be willing to obey whether the handler uses the leash, or not.

How Collar and Leash Training Works

If you choose to train your dog focusing on collar and leash training, it's important to use the training collar and the lead properly. The reason? The training hinges on the pressure applied by the training collar – which is designed to apply varying degrees of pressure – whenever the leash is tightened. The pressure you convey through the leash then becomes the pressure conveyed through the training collar. The collar is adjustable to vary the pressure, according to the dog's response.

The variability of pressure lets you adjust the pressure in

accordance with the dog's response to the training; different dogs respond differently, so a flexible pressure is useful. For example, the first time your dog encounters the collar and leash, he may fight it and take a bit of time to adjust to it, while other dogs might not react strongly at all. In this approach to training, it's important to note how your dog reacts, and adapt the pressure and training program accordingly.

Begin by purchasing a quality training collar that fits your dog. There are a number of collars and leashes to choose from. Don't skimp on this purchase; imagine chasing your dog as he runs toward a busy street, and you'll understand why it's important to purchase quality products that won't break and result in your dog running free and out of your control.

Measure the circumference of your dog's neck, and purchase a collar about 2" larger. In measuring, the measuring tape should not be loose, but neither should it be tight and snug against the dog's neck.

Go larger rather than smaller – most of the collars you'll find are offered in even-numbered sizes, so round the size up if your measurement is an odd number of inches (i.e., if your dog's neck measures 7" and the collar you want is offered in even numbers, purchase an 8" collar rather than a 6" one). The chain that attaches to the training collar should be located at the top of your dog's neck to apply the correct pressure.

The training collar is an effective training tool because it is designed to apply pressure in varying degrees and to relieve the applied pressure instantly. Using it requires the handler to become familiar with the collar; some styles are easy to use, and some require more finesse. If you need help choosing, a professional trainer or an informed pet store manager should be able to help you choose the appropriate collar. Then, your first step is to become familiar with the collar and how it works. Examine it and note how the collar will tighten when you tug on the leash.

Once you've familiarized yourself with the collar and how it works, you are ready to begin using it to train your dog to walk on a lead. Your goal here is to train your dog to walk at your side, with a loose lead. He should keep his head relatively even with your knee, and never charge ahead of you or lag behind. So your dog will need to be able to vary his pace to match yours. Never vary your pace to match the dog's pace; the goal is for the dog to adjust to you, not vice versa.

If your dog does lag behind, or pull ahead of you, immediately correct him by tugging quickly on the leash, to remind him to adjust his pace. Immediately loosen the leash to relieve the pressure as soon as he responds.

The beauty of the training collar and leash is that most dogs respond immediately to a slight correction. If your dog does not respond, it may be because he has built up the muscles in his neck from preexisting behavior problems. In that case, the dog needs greater correction, and you will need to apply greater pressure. If, after applying greater pressure, your dog is still not responding well, check to see the training collar is large enough. You may want to ask a trainer for help at this point, to understand what is holding your training back.

Teaching a Puppy to Accept His Collar and Leash

The first step in training your puppy - and the most important – is that he learn to walk using a collar and leash. He must be comfortable wearing the collar and leash for subsequent training to be effective, and, indeed, for them to be possible at all.

Some puppies – not many – accept the collar and leash with no problems. If yours does not, don't worry. It's a process. Follow these steps, and in a short time, your puppy will accept the leash and collar and be ready for what training comes next.

Find the right collar for your puppy – one that fits, and is not too light or too heavy, not too thick and not too thin. The first step toward getting the puppy to accept the collar and leash is to find a collar that fits the dog properly. It is important that the collar be neither too light (or it could break) nor too heavy (uncomfortable to wear), and neither too thin nor too thick.

To determine the correct collar size, measure the circumference of your dog's neck, and purchase a collar about 2" larger. In measuring, the measuring tape should not be loose, but neither should it be tight and snug against the dog's neck.

Most collars are sized in two-inch increments, so you may have to round up to get a properly sized collar. For instance, if the dog has a 13" neck, you would buy a 14" collar, and so on.

Once you have the right collar, you are ready to put it on your puppy. Do this in the safest environment – your home. You're just going to let the puppy wear the collar around the house. Don't worry if your puppy is stressed and unhappy at wearing the collar, and whines or tries to pull it off. This is normal behavior. You should neither punish him, not comfort him. Just ignore him and let him work through his issues on his own.

Be patient – let the puppy wear the collar for a number of days, without taking it off, so he'll get used to the feel of it. After several days have passed and the puppy has completely adjusted, you are ready to begin working with the leash.

Choose a lightweight leash. Again – have the puppy at home,

attach the leash to the collar, and simply let the puppy wander around the house, getting used to the feel of leash and collar. Stay nearby, but give him room to wander on his own. Be sure he doesn't get caught on furniture or other objects, as getting snagged could frighten him and delay your progress.

When you begin training, only attach the leash for a short time – a few minutes or so. Do it during times the puppy is happy – when you are playing, when it's mealtime, etc. Even when it isn't attached, keep the leash near the puppy's water bowl, so he can investigate it when he wants, become familiar with it, and realize it isn't something he needs to fear.

If you follow these initial steps and are patient, your dog should soon become used to walking through the house with the leash attached. Now he's ready for the next step. Attach the leash, and after a moment, take the end of it in your hand and hold it. You are not trying to walk your dog, or direct him in any way – you're simply holding the leash and letting the dog go where he will, with you following, leash in hand.

Avoid letting the leash go taut. Give your dog a good experience with this step, by calling him to you as you hold the leash, and if he comes, getting lots of praise and a tasty treat. Whatever happens, just allow your puppy to react in whatever way he does, and to move as he wants. You are letting him get used to the feel of the collar and leash when you are holding the end of the leash.

Again, take your time with this step, as future success will depend on you giving the puppy time to get used to the feel of the collar and leash before you attempt to lead him. Still keep this initial "getting used to it" period in places your dog feels safe – probably, your home.

Once the dog feels comfortable and confident, try letting him get used to the feel of the collar and leash outside. Start small – choose an enclosed backyard or small patio space that is outdoors, but protected and familiar. Make it a very short exercise, especially in the beginning. You can stretch the time out visit by visit. When the time is right, take your puppy around the neighborhood, with the collar on and the leash in your hand. He'll have a chance to meet neighbors for a bit of socialization, and you can begin to help him learn to deal with distractions.

Take your puppy's characteristics into consideration as you decide how quickly to move forward with these training steps. Some puppies take to collar and leash training as though they've been wearing a collar and leash from the first day they began to walk around and explore; others take more time. Be cognizant of what your puppy needs to feel safe and confident.

If your puppy looks like he's developing a habit of chewing on his leash, discourage him by putting a bad-tasting substance like bitter apple or Tabasco sauce on the leash. Make sure whatever you choose is not toxic.

Collar and leash training is a required basic for any further work you'll do with your dog. No dog should ever be taken outside, where it might interact with other animals or with people, without wearing a collar and leash. Even if your dog is Mr. Friendly and a threat to no one, you can't control the actions of others. If a child unwittingly rushes your dog, or another dog lunges at you, it's important that you have control. And of course, a collar that has on it tags that give your contact information is a precaution that will help you get your dog back, should the unexpected happen and he ends up far from home.

During the early stages of leash and collar training, remember to give your dog all the time he needs to get fully comfortable with the collar, and then the leash. If he pulls at it, turns circles or otherwise acts unhappy, just leave him alone to make his peace with it – he will, in time. Never punish him for playing with the collar, or resisting it. Instead, try distracting him with a toy, an offer to play, or a favorite treat.

Training Your Dog to Not Pull On the Leash

Owners often struggle with their dog pulling on their leash. No doubt you've seen someone out with their dog who is being walked by the dog, rather than the other way around (hopefully you haven't experienced that shameful situation yourself!).

It's important to address leash pulling, not just because it makes time with your dog less pleasant, but because it's a safety issue. Constant pulling on the leash can lead to the collar or leash breaking, or the leash slipping from your hand; now you have a headstrong, excitable dog running free, which is a danger to the dog and to others. Pulling can also put you, as the handler, in a dangerous situation if the dog sets out running, and you are running behind.

A dog who pulls on the leash may be excitable and unable to control that excitability. Or he may be having authority issues, unwilling to give your control as the "alpha" in your relationship. If your dog begins to pull on the leash out of excitability, give him a chance to calm down; just stand quietly for a minute or two until the situation passes, or the dog moves beyond being excited and reactive.

If your dog is asserting dominance, however, that's an indication you may need to do some retraining, as it's essential to your relationship that you have the dominant role. You have to have the dog's respect at all times for the training you're doing to be effective.

When your dog attempts to be the dominant one in your relationship, step back and review the basic commands until the dog is entirely compliant and obedient. You may find that a formal training school , or a formal approach to re-training, is helpful. You should also consider getting advice from a trainer on what you, as handler, may be doing to exacerbate the situation. Often, an inexperienced handler is responding from instinct, and those responses can complicate the alpha handler/obedient dog relationship you want.

You want a dog that is calm and accepting of the collar and lead. Set the tone before you even attach the collar. It's natural for your dog to be excited that you're going for a walk together but establish control by insisting (gently) that the dog calm down and sit still for you to put the collar on him. If he wiggles, gets up while you're putting it on, or gets up without your permission once it's on, immediately put him back in a "sit." You should only move on to walking with him once he sits calmly until you release him from the "sit."

Ensure his calm obedience continues as you walk to the door. Any jumping or pulling should be addressed by immediately putting your dog back in a "sit/stay." Once the dog has obeyed and is calm, move toward the door again, but if he acts up, repeat the sit/stay until he walks calmly with you, in the correct position (head level with your knee).

Nor should the dog pull and surge once you reach the door. If that happens, go back into the house and close the door behind you, and repeat the whole sit/stay process until he can do so calmly. It's important to start your walk completely in control.

Calm and control are vital; so is focus. Your dog should be focused on you, your needs and commands at all times. His behavior should be based on your guidance — not on his own impulses and desires. You can reinforce this dynamic by starting and stopping the walk frequently, with the expectation that your dog will also immediately and responsively stop and automatically sit. Train yourself (yes, this is about training you in good habits, too!) to ask the dog to stop and immediately sit, whenever you stop during the walk. That will train your dog to keep his focus on you.

When you are walking and come to a stop, check to be sure your dog is focused on you, and that he immediately sits. Then begin to walk forward again. If the dog surges ahead, come to an abrupt stop and command your dog to sit. Repeat, taking only a few steps, until the dog is automatically staying by your side, focused on you as you walk, and automatically and immediately sitting when you stop. Then remember the final requirement — praise and/or reward for obedience!

Never continue to walk your dog if he pulls on the leash. If you do, you have actually rewarded him for bad behavior. A good way to think of it is this: your dog is learning how to behave, whether you are consciously teaching him or not. If he learns the wrong things now, you will both have a lot more work to do to learn the right things, and the right way, later.

Be consistently consistent. Any time your dog surges ahead – whether during initial training, or two years down the road – immediately stop and put him into a sit. Keep him in the sit until he focuses on you, and hold the sit and the focus for a few seconds before you set out again.

Taking Your Dog Training Off Leash

There is a real sense of freedom and pleasure for many dog owners once their dog is trained well enough to take him off leash. Do yourself a favor and don't move off leash until your dog is utterly compliant and obedient. Wait until the dog has mastered all the basic commands – sit, stay, call on command, etc. – on leash, before trying it off leash.

Even if your dog is behaving perfectly, exercise caution the first few times you go off leash. As with the other training, begin in a safe and familiar environment, such as the fenced backyard of your home. Think of it this way: you've been working with a strong and reliable instrument of control, a leash. You are now removing that control. Your dog needs to obey your voice commands as unthinkingly and reliably as he would behave if he were on a leash.

So the first few times you take your dog off leash, it shouldn't be in a high-traffic area. Test him in a safe environment to be sure – absolutely sure – that he will obey your voice commands each and every time.

Your training should focus on de-sensitizing your dog to distractions. For example, place your dog in a safe environment, such as your fenced backyard. With your dog on a leash, command him to sit by your side (head in line with your knee). Then test him with distractions, such as other people walking by, or walking their dog in close proximity. Watch how your dog reacts. He should remain sitting and focused; if he pulls on the leash, immediately put him into the sit/stay again.

You should repeat this exercise until you see your dog is remaining in the sit/stay despite distractions. Then try the distractions, holding the leash at first and then dropping it. Your dog should remain in the sit/stay. Once you've completed that exercise several times, successfully, perform it off-leash entirely. Test the dog by tempting him with a variety of distractions – cats, rolling balls, noise, etc.

Now move on to trying other basic commands, off leash, and

with distractions. For example, invite a couple of neighbors and their dogs over. As the dogs begin to play with each other, call your dog to come to you; praise him when he does. Let him return to playing, and call him again. The point here is that no matter what he is interested in, his own interests are put aside when you give a command and convey an expectation. Remember – as always, when he obeys, give him lots of praise and/or a treat for a reward.

Next, practice in a really distracting spot that is fenced to ensure your dog's safety, such as a dog park. Let your dog play and sniff at will; but when you call him to you, he should come immediately. Praise him, and let him return to playing; then call him again. This will teach your dog to come to you when called, no matter what, and letting him return to what he enjoys will get him in the habit of obeying you with the expectation that he can probably return to his activities, once you release him to do that.

When your dog consistently obeys you, immediately, with the basic commands off-leash, you can consider him ready to be off leash, but never unsupervised. Many owners have assumed good behavior means the dog will never disobey or react inappropriately, only to regret that assumption when the dog gets in trouble. Be a responsible owner; train your dog well, but remain engaged and attentive to possible dangers.

Chapter 6: Head Collar Training

Head collar training is an increasingly popular approach to training dogs. It's sometimes a good choice with dogs that are stubborn, physically strong, or particularly dominant.

Advantages of Head Collars

The advantages of head collar training over collar/leash training are:

Beginning trainers and handlers often find head collars easier to use, and more effective

Head collars can be more effective at correcting, restraining and controlling a dog that tends to pull

The head collar offers more control with dogs that are stronger

Head collars give added assurance of control in situations that are particularly distracting, such as areas where there are other dogs or high traffic

Don't make the mistake of thinking the extra control head collars give is a substitute for good training. But a dog that's been trained well, and has a head collar too, gives you a strong chance of controlling the dog in any situation.

Disadvantages of Head Collars

Those advantages aside, the head collar also has disadvantages.

- A clever dog may adjust its behavior depending on whether he's wearing the head collar or a regular collar. This sets a bad precedent; your goal is for your dog to respond to commands consistently, whatever the circumstances or equipment.

- The head collar is particularly irritating to some dogs. As with de-sensitizing your dog to a regular collar and leash, the approach should be to leave the dog to his own devices until he accepts the collar, while you watch to ensure he's safe.

- Another disadvantage is not in relation to the dog but in people's response to the head collar. The look of the head collar suggests to some people that the dog is a biter, and can result in negative interactions.

Even with its disadvantages, a head collar can be a useful tool, particularly with strong or stubborn dogs. Its value largely depends on using it according to the manufacturer's recommendations, and with solid training approaches

Chapter 7: Reward Training

Though reward training may seem like the newest thing, it's actually likely to be the oldest method of training in use today. Some think that it was what early humans used to domesticate wolf pups, to become the family companion animals our dogs are today.

Understanding the Wolf Pack

It's likely that some kind of training that involves reward for obedience has been a part of humans' relationship with their dogs for thousands of years. Why should that matter to you, as a trainer/owner/handler today? Because your dog comes from a long line of dogs that were descended from wolves, and much of the behavioral characteristics of the wolf is still hard-wired in your dog today. Understanding the behavior of a wolf with its pack leader helps you understand the behavior of your dog in relation to his pack leader – you.

How did wolves become domesticated and begin to evolve into the animals we have today? A few thousand years ago, humans probably tamed wolf pups to be used for protection from human and animal predators and to notify the tribe, by their barking, when danger was near. They may have begun with orphaned or abandoned pups that looked to humans to survive.

It's also very possible the animals were valued for the same things we value them for today – their ability to be insightful companions, their loyal and loving natures. That relationship also meant that dogs with the ability to relate best to humans were valued and fed, so they survived and passed along to their offspring those strong relationship skills. Over the centuries, as the relationship between dogs and humans evolved, humans began to train and use dogs for such complex jobs as herding.

Wolf packs are formed and function on hierarchy within the pack. The image of the "lone wolf" may be appealing, but the truth is, wolves do not generally survive well on their own. They need a pack for a number of reasons, not the least of which is that they hunt better, and eat better when they are members of a pack. So it was to a wolf's advantage to learn to function within a pack – indeed, his survival often depended on that ability.

In the hierarchy of the pack, each member knows, quite clearly, his or her place and function. The hierarchy is fixed, for the most part; it only changes if a wolf dies or is injured, or occasionally when there is a struggle for one wolf to take the pack over from another.

That heritage means your dog's nature is to look to a pack leader for discipline, guidance, and reward. The leader of a wolf pack calls the shots, yes, but he also provides food, leadership, protection, and affection. And that, in a nutshell, is the basis of reward training – or any good approach to dog training. The handler – man or woman – establishes themselves as the pack leader, and the dog looks to them for its needs.

Your dog will be happier and more well-balanced if you understand and provide a home and relationship that is similar to what your dog would have as a member of a wolf pack. There are some dogs that are stubborn – but most dogs need and value a leader. It makes them feel safe and secure, and your dog is hard-wired to be subservient, obedient and affectionate to a strong pack leader.

That said, some dogs, and certain breeds, are easily dominated, and others less so. Even within your dog's littermates, there were some that were leaders and some that were followers. You can spot this if you observe puppies with their siblings; the dominant and submissive personalities are easy to recognize. For your purposes, it's important to remember, when choosing a puppy, that you'll find a dog who has a more submissive personality easier to train, especially if you are using positive reinforcement; a more submissive puppy will not be as likely to challenge your leadership, and in fact, will welcome it.

Reward Training Today

While the approach to reward training is a rather ancient one, today's version of reward training has experienced an upsurge in support over the past decade or two. In deciding what approach you want to use with your dog, you should know that, while many believe dogs should be trained only with reward training, the best approach is often reward training combined with leash/collar training.

Remember that dogs respond differently to different training approaches – some do well with reward training, some respond not at all to reward training but take to leash/collar training easily. Experiment with training approaches, and decide which is best for your dog.

Also keep in mind that training based on rewards is often the best approach to training a dog that has been abused, or has behavior problems. Reward training is the best training to establish a strong bond between you and a dog that is resistant to having that bond with you.

Another thing to consider is how thoroughly and complexly you plan to train your dog. Reward training relies on using some form of food as a reward for obedience. More complex behaviors can generally only be taught with reward training, which is why people who train dogs to do complex jobs, or to perform in movies, are likely to use reward training. It's the go-to approach for those training dogs for police and military work, too, particularly when scent detection and tracking are the goal.

But reward training is effective with basic obedience commands, too. It's based on getting the dog to perform of its own free will, in order to get something the dog desires, usually food — although the positive reinforcement is sometimes provided in the form of praise. This training results in a dog that is well-trained and who will perform without being touched.

If you've heard of clicker training, that is a form of reward training. Like other forms of training, it's more effective for some dogs than for others. In this training, the dog learns to associate a clicking sound with a reward (a treat, or praise). In time, with repetition, the dog learns to respond with the clicker alone.

Just know that, whatever type of dog you have, and whatever its challenges or idiosyncrasies, it's almost certain that you can train him well, enjoyably and successfully with training that relies on positive reinforcement. It's a method that fosters respect and trust between handler and animal, rather than relying on intimidation and fear, and that's the best way to get the most from your dog, or any dog.

Ensuring your Dog is Reliable

Because dogs trained with the reward training approach often have a job to do, such as working as a police dog, it's vital that the dog is reliable. Here are some guidelines:

- Get the dog accustomed to working around distractions.

- Properly socialize your dog, both to other animals and to people.

- Once your dog has settled into the training, train at a variety of locations. You have to take the dog outside its area of comfort to be sure he's reliable in any environment.

- As part of the training, teach the dog to focus on its handler. If you have your dog's attention, it's much easier to have control. One of the advantages of reward training is that, when used properly, it gains the attention and respect of the dog.

Rewarding with Treats

Trainers in all walks of life – those who train police dogs, animal for films or circus, and others – have found that animals respond well to rewards that are food-based. An added plus is that this type of training is generally accomplished more quickly.

See if that's true for your dog as well, by testing his response to food as motivation. Around the time he generally eats, take a piece of food and move it around, close to his nose. Does your dog respond, and seem enthusiastic? If so, this would be a good time of day to train with rewards. If the dog does not respond, you may need to select another time, or another form of training, or delay dinnertime to get more enthusiasm and interest.

It's generally a good idea to feed your dog at a set time and take up any uneaten food to set a routine and prevent obesity. But in particular, feed at a set time and don't leave food out if you are using reward training; otherwise, your dog may not be motivated enough for the training to be effective.

Teaching the "Come When Called" Command

If you've tested your dog to gauge his interest in food, and gotten a positive response, that's the sign to proceed with reward training. Be ready to initiate the lesson when the dog shows an interest in his food. Give him a piece of food; then hold out another piece and back away a step or two, saying "come here." When the dog follows the food and comes closer to you, praise him and reward him with the food.

Once your dog understands the command and begins coming to you automatically and easily, add a step — call him to you as before, but add a "sit" command, and hold his collar for a few seconds before giving him the food. This is the basis for a number of other trainings you can choose to give, such as performing tricks or executing more difficult commands.

At the next level of training, the three-step "come/sit/stay" training will give your dog a skill that's useful to you in a number of situations. Begin by walking with your dog; stop, and the dog should sit, as it's been trained to do. Give your dog a few moments in the "sit," and then, turning to face your dog, say "stay" and begin to back away (note, you are facing your dog, each of you looking at the other, as you take steps backward to move away from him). Repeat this step until the dog stays throughout the exercise.

Once he accomplishes that, back away with him in a "stay" — then call him to you. This is an exercise/training of several steps, so when your dog masters it and comes to you after a solid sit/stay, praise him enthusiastically! This is the kind of performance and ability you want from him — let him know what a good job he did. That tells him what your expectations are, and tells him how to respond next time. Plus — he worked hard, obeyed, and deserves the praise.

You may be tempted to take on more challenges because it's fun to see your dog respond and succeed, but remember training sessions should not become tiresome or boring for your dog.

Keep them short, especially in the beginning. You'll also want to be sure you aren't giving so many treats as rewards that your dog begins to gain too much weight. Most dogs enjoy the time with you when you are training, and once the treats have helped you indicate to your dog what you want from him, you can scale back on them – he'll perform just for the joy of pleasing you. Continue to provide treats – that's an important motivator – but you don't have to provide them as often.

The "stop/sit/stay/come" exercise is a terrific base exercise for a number of games and additional training. Your dog is now obeying well off-leash, so you can go to places where he can run free, although, remember it's still important to keep him in safe environments –fenced, and away from traffic or other dangers. Introduce him to different locations – a dog park, if he's good with other dogs, or a friend's backyard, perhaps for a play date with their dog. In the midst of his play, call him to come to you. Praise him extensively when he does, rubbing and scratching him in his favorite places as you tell him what a good dog he is. Your goal is to make him so happy that coming to you when you call is something he wants to do, no matter what.

Note: some dog trainers and handlers advise against going to dog parks; your dog may function well there, but you don't know how well other dogs and owners you encounter will do. The dog park can offer a lot of fun for you and your dog, but know your dog's temperament and capabilities, and if you choose to take your dog to a dog park, watch carefully when you're there.

Relying on Positive Reinforcement

Many owners and handlers – including professional handlers of police dogs, military dogs, and dogs who perform for television and movies – swear by the effectiveness of positive reinforcement training with rewards. Such training generally leads to an enjoyable experience for both dog and handler and results in a skilled companion dog that is responsive and obedient.

What makes positive reinforcement training effective is that the rewards teach the dog what you expect. The reward makes it clear to the dog that what he just did was what you wanted him to do. The reward is often food – especially in the early stages of training – but as training progresses, a good scratch behind his ears or enthusiastic praising works well with most dogs. Just remember – reward him in some way, not just at the beginning of training, but throughout training and, indeed, throughout your life with him as your companion.

Chapter 8: Unwanted Behavior

We've covered the basics of dog training, and gone into particular approaches. If all has gone well, you and your dog have sailed right through the training and your dog is responding to a number of commands, reliably and well.

And it may be that the training is running into some challenges. Here are some guidelines for what to do when you encounter dog training issues or unwanted behaviors.

Your Dog's Instinctive Response to Authority

A well-trained dog is a superior companion whose training keeps him, and others, safe from harm. The training can truly be a factor of life or death, for both your dog and for others that his behavior might impact. It's no accident that many professional trainers are most often called in to address a dog who is aggressive, and who can't interact properly with the family, other humans, or other animals.

Ironically, understanding your dog's genetic background as a wild creature will help you understand how to better domesticate him into the obedient companion animal that will be rewarding to both of you.

The beginning of dogs' domestication was likely when orphaned wolf cubs were adopted by early humans. The relationship wasn't too far from what it is today – the dogs were appealing, loving, loyal. They needed food and shelter, and humans provided that in return for things the dogs could provide that the humans valued, such as support in hunting, help driving off predators, and serving as early warning signals when danger was approaching. Today, working and herding dogs, police dogs and dog performers still perform valuable work for their human owners.

You'll have a better instinct about training your dog and respond to challenges better when you remember your dog's background as a member of a pack. Wild dogs and wolves form packs with a specific hierarchy. Every animal in the pack knows his place in that hierarchy and knows what to expect in terms of the associated responsibilities and expected behaviors.

The entire pack defers to the leadership of the alpha dog. The alpha makes the call on choices around hunting, food, and whether to avoid other animals or engage in conflict with them. To our human minds, it might seem the alpha dog was an enemy to be overcome; but in truth, pack members feel confident and relaxed when they have a strong alpha leader they can trust. Your dog will be more stable and happier if you are a strong alpha leader for him. He will see you as a superior, and will follow your commands – the more he perceives you as alpha, the more likely he is to follow commands quickly and without question.

Dog Training for Desired Behaviors

It just makes sense that it's easier to train your dog in the behaviors you want than it is to correct bad behavior. So do you and your dog a favor – invest in quality training time with him, on a regular basis.

That's especially true when you have a young dog. It's not all work – as we've said, even when you have unstructured play time with your puppy, he's learning. But it's also important to engage in formal training to teach your puppy what you expect from him, and which behaviors are acceptable to you, and which are not.

If you take the time to teach these lessons when your puppy is young, it's more likely he'll learn them quickly, and retain the lessons. Remember – every experience your puppy has teaches him something. Make sure his experiences are teaching him well and reinforcing the things you want him to know, and the behaviors you want to see.

The strong bond that dogs form with humans is one of your biggest assets in training your dog. That bond is based on relationships humans have had with dogs for thousands of years; the dog's ability to form that relationship made his survival more likely, so the qualities of respect, affection and obedience were preserved just by virtue of natural selection.

Also useful in your approaches to training your dog are the dynamics of pack hierarchy, and your position as the leader of your dog's pack. Make it a point to use that hierarchy when you train your dog. In setting yourself up as the leader of your dog's pack, you gain his trust and his respect. Conversely, if your dog does not recognize you as his superior, and a leader worthy of his respect, your training will be much more difficult, if not impossible.

How do you gain and keep that respect? It can't be forced. Rather, it is earned by your interactions with your dog. Using the reward or positive reinforcement approach to training teaches the dog to respect you and trust you, far more than he would if you based your interactions on fear and intimidation. As noted previously – fear causes your dog to exhibit aggressive behavior, such as biting.

Because of that, punishing your dog only frightens and confuses him; one bad episode can set your training back weeks, even months. It's an interactive process to train your dog well, giving him the option to choose to do what you ask of him, and rewarding him with praise, treats or other positive elements when he makes the right decision. If, for example, your dog chases people, arrange to have a friend jog past while you have your dog on leash. Your dog has a choice: he can refrain from chasing the jogger, and if he does, you should reward him. If he chases him, sit him back down and start the exercise again, until he understands.

It isn't about punishing him for the wrong decision. It is about rewarding him for choosing to respond in accordance with what you want from him. Always keep in mind that rewarding your dog, rather than punishing him, will be far more likely to result in a well-trained – and happy – dog, and a satisfied owner.

Your Dog's Motivation for Behaving Badly

There are a number of reasons why people train their dogs. There are practical reasons, such as ensuring the safety of the dog and those around him. But there are softer reasons as well – the joy that a well-trained dog and its owner find in each other, the companionship, loyalty, and love.

Bad behavior doesn't usually indicate your dog is a hopeless miscreant. If you take the time to understand the reason for his behaviors and address them accordingly, you can still have the companion animal you want him to be – it just may take a bit more time and effort. For example, it's easy to be frustrated when your dog chews your new furniture; it's easier to understand his behavior if you realize it's in response to his separation anxiety. In training to offset bad behaviors, it's important to address the root cause – the anxiety – rather than the behavior itself – the chewing.

In fact, very often your dog's behavior may look aggressive or thoughtless, but it's in response to his inability to cope with anxiety. You might think you need to reduce the stress he feels, and certainly that's helpful; but more often, the best approach is to engage in a training program that teaches him to better tolerate and deal with the stress.

By now, you've probably observed that what motivates a human, and human behavior, can be very different from the things that motivate a dog, and dog behavior. And from what you've read so far, you may have come to the realization that a good handler doesn't just train his dog in good behavior – he's also training himself to be the kind of trainer that leads to having an obedient dog. When trying to understand your dog's behavior, don't confuse his motivations with those of a human. Sure, he may seem almost human at times, particularly if he's especially intelligent. But even if he understands things in the way a human would, his motivations are different, as are his responses to situations and challenges.

So modulate your thinking and your behaviors to remember that your dog is a dog – not a human. Just as you remember the things humans and dogs share – the need for relationships and close bonds with those in the pack family.

Refusing to Come when Called

If your relationship with your dog isn't all you'd like, take a moment to ask if your problems hearken back to your dog's training on coming when you call. Not only does "come when called" impact a number of other behaviors; failing to come when he's called to you can result in dangerous situations you're unprepared for, such as having a collar break near heavy traffic, or your dog bolting and getting free to chase a person or a cat. Consider for a moment the possible legal repercussions of your dog's failure to come when called, or the possibility that his uncontrolled impulsiveness could actually prove fatal to him.

Your dog learns from what he's allowed to do. When you allow him to run off leash and indulge himself in whatever behavior he likes, you're damaging any training you've done that teaches him to look to you – not himself – for what he does and the choices he makes. Running loose in a park, or on the beach, or with other dogs is fun; probably more fun than things you'd rather he was doing. Some dogs can handle free time, are aware when the handler is changing the parameters to be about obedience, and can adjust. If your dog cannot adjust, you need to limit how much free, impulsive time he has to practice behaviors and choices that don't involve your commands.

You can understand, if you put yourself in your dog's place. Picture him doing the things he loves, like running wild on the beach – imagine you're the dog, for a second. The waves are rolling in, you're chasing them, there are other dogs running free, and you're chasing them too, and roughhousing with them. And – oh, no. Here comes your handler, wanting you to obey, for Pete's sake. Taking the fun out of everything. Killjoy! Seen from that perspective, you can understand why a dog might grow resistant to leash, collar, and training.

What to do? One likely approach your dog might take is just to ignore you when you call and refusing to come. And now you're in a rough spot because your dog has learned there's a reward for him – fun, and freedom – in ignoring you.

If your dog has not yet realized the potential ignoring you has, do yourself a favor and don't let him learn it. It's a lot easier to prevent this learned behavior than it is to work with him to un-learn it.

If he has already learned it – as is likely, if you're reading this section of the book – your approach should be to supervise his play and make the time you spend with your dog fun, so he associates your call with something positive, rather than with something that limits his good time.

You won't reprogram your dog by following "Come" with something unpleasant, so try not to do that. Don't call him and then give him a bath, clip his nails or do something else he really doesn't like, or you'll be teaching him if he comes when called, he's going to regret it.

Instead, call him and then give him a toy, a treat, or some playtime with you. Use some other command to get his attention when there's something unpleasant in store for him.

Remember – your dog is constantly learning. He's learning when you're training him in obedience – but he's also learning when you call him, and he comes and is sorry, and learning when he's having fun and you call him and he ignores you – the fun continues. So approach your relationship with him as though every interaction is laying the groundwork you want to secure his attention and his obedience.

And remember the key to training him – positive reinforcement. Just make it a habit to reward your dog each and every time he shows the behavior and obedience you want. Certainly, if you're having training issues, you may need to rely on treats that are irresistible – generally, yummy bits of tasty food. But dogs are sensitive to energy, so the reward can be a simple scratch behind the ears or a "Yeah, good boy!" When teaching the dog to come on command, it is vital that the dog be consistently rewarded every single time he does as the owner wants. A reward can be as simple as a pat on the head, a "good boy" or a scratch behind the ears. Whatever the reward, be consistent in giving something positive every time you call your dog and he comes.

Eliminating Biting Behaviors

Puppies are impulsive and enthusiastic. Those qualities are what make them such a joy – and can also make them challenging. Puppies are prone to chewing and biting. Here are some approaches to curbing biting behaviors.

Preventing Biting and Mouthing

Puppies and young dogs are often prone to biting and mouthing. It's natural for a puppy to bite and mouth its siblings when playing, and when you play with your puppy, it's natural for him to play that way with you, too. But puppies have thick skin; humans do not, and those sharp little puppy teeth can be a problem. So it's important to let your puppy know when his approaches to playing with you are appropriate, and when they are not.

A puppy's mother and its siblings would ordinarily teach him what biting behavior is appropriate, and what is not. But since puppies are now taken away from their mothers at a younger age, your puppy may have missed out on that mother/puppy training.

So it's up to you to train your puppy by inhibiting his reflex to bite. Don't let biting continue just because it's not a big problem now; your little 5-pound puppy is going to grow, and what is a small problem now could very well become a big problem later. To ensure your adult dog won't have biting and mouthing problems, teach your puppy to control his urge to bite before he reaches the age of four months.

You can tap back into the natural way of teaching the puppy, by letting him interact and socialize with older dogs or other active puppies. If you've watched puppies with other puppies and dogs, you'll notice they bite each other almost constantly when playing. The puppies are testing limits; they bite harder until another puppy or dog reacts in a negative way, growling or snapping or biting back. That's how a puppy learns what's appropriate and acceptable, and what isn't. Through this kind of play, your puppy will learn some of the lessons that help him control his biting reflex. Even so — his little teeth don't hurt the thicker skin of other dogs and puppies the same way it will hurt a human, so you may need to give him additional lessons in what's appropriate with you.

Using Trust to Prevent Biting

The more your puppy trusts and respects you, the less problem you're likely to have with biting. At the least, a trusting and respectful relationship will let you address biting problems more easily and effectively. Indeed, all dog training is impacted by the level of trust and respect your dog has for you.

Your dog's level of trust in you is severely damaged if and when you hit or slap it. The reason this book emphasizes training that is positive and rewarding is that it fosters a trusting relationship and bond between dog and owner – and that relationship, in turn, makes training easier and more effective. Nothing erodes your relationship with your dog like physical punishment. In terms of biting behaviors, reprimanding your dog for biting may be your first instinct, but it will only scare and confuse your dog, and it won't do anything to alter his behavior. Stay positive with your training – always.

Eliminating Bad Habits

If you have a dog or puppy, it's like any relationship – there will be times that things don't go quite as you'd like them to. Any owner of a dog or puppy will sometimes find themselves needing to work with the dog to alter behavior of some sort.

Most dogs love their owner and see him or her as their pack leader; a dog's nature is to want to please their pack leader, and dogs are sufficiently smart enough to do so if you clearly communicate what is acceptable and unacceptable. In other words, your dog will very likely do what you want him to do, providing he knows and understands what you expect.

The approach to shifting unwanted behavior depends on the behavior itself, and, to some extent, the nature and character of your dog. Each dog is different; there are similarities among dogs of a certain breed, of course, but even so, each dog is an individual, and you may need to try a couple of approaches before you find the best approach to eliminating unwanted behavior.

Whining, Howling and Excessive Barking

Dogs are usually vocal, and in fact, were almost certainly valued for their ability to bark and warn humans of danger. Both dogs and puppies are natural barkers and may howl and whine, and that's normal. But at some point, it can become a problem. It's particularly challenging if you live in an apartment or home very close to your neighbor. Your neighbors have a right to expect that your dog won't always be disturbing their peace with the sounds he makes.

What to do? Here are some tips to control excessive barking and other vocalizations:

- Your dog may be whining to tell you it truly needs something; for example, if your dog or puppy is crated and begins to howl or whine, take it to its toilet area. The dog may be letting you know it needs to do its business.

- In addition to needing to relieve itself, the dog may be whining for other reasons, so check to be sure he has water and isn't ill. Check to see his toy isn't out of reach under a chair, and that the temperature isn't too hot or cold.

- In addition to physical needs, be sure your dog is getting all the affection and attention he needs to feel confident and loved. Also, make sure he has toys to keep himself occupied.

- Training emphasizes building a bond by spending time together, but there are times (perhaps often) that your dog will need to be left in the home alone. It's part of pack behavior for your dog to want you to be with him, and if you are gone, he may suffer from separation anxiety, which can lead to such behaviors as destroying furniture and incessant barking. Work to accustom your puppy to being left alone.

- Be careful that in being responsive to your dog's needs, you don't inadvertently reward him for unwanted behavior. For example, if he whines, don't go to him and give him attention –

that only reinforces his tendency to whine. Instead, once you've made sure his physical needs are met and that he is comfortable and has what he needs by way of toys, it is appropriate to scold him for whining, letting him know that whining is unwanted behavior.

Problem Chewing

Just as you can expect your puppy to vocalize, you can also expect him to chew. Puppies use their mouth, tongue, and teeth to explore their world. Just because chewing is normal, however, that doesn't mean it's acceptable behavior; "normal" is not a reason to be OK with your puppy chewing your new leather boots. Address unwanted chewing early, so your chewing puppy doesn't become a big, chewing dog.

Chewing itself is OK, and it's fine to encourage your dog to chew appropriate items, such as his toys. Giving your dog a variety of chew toys helps keep him entertained, makes him feel safe in that he can satisfy a need in a way that is acceptable, and help him keep his teeth and gums clean and exercised.

To reinforce the "OK to chew/not OK to chew" guideline for your puppy, encourage him to play with his chew toys. Praise him for playing with them and chewing with them. If you find him chewing something inappropriate, gently take it away, and hand him a toy; then praise him when he pays attention to and chews the toy.

Another way you can encourage him to play with his toys and chew them, and let him know you approve, is to take advantage of his enthusiasm when he greets you. As you come in the door and the puppy runs to you, put your things down, hand him one of his toys, and praise him for taking it. You can also encourage him to go get one of his toys every time he greets you.

Your puppy's toys should be easily accessible; he will probably be drawn to chew on anything and everything that's accessible all his life, so keep things picked up and out of his reach. In particular, try to keep things that carry your scent – shoes, hairbrushes, used tissues – out of his reach.

If you witness your puppy picking up something he shouldn't have, such as a sock, distract him with another toy as you take the sock away. When he takes the toy, be sure to praise him for playing with it and chewing on it.

If the chewing continues, you can try taking an item you are certain the dog knows you do not want him to chew; putting something bad-tasting but non-toxic on it, such as hot pepper sauce; and leaving it for him to find. The unpleasant reaction he has should help train him to only chew on items you've told him are appropriate.

Jumping On People

You've probably been jumped on by a friend's dog, and wish you hadn't been. It's a common behavior, and one owners often express a wish to change. Changing this behavior is certainly possible, but it's harder to change it if you encouraged it when your puppy was young, and only now find it less appealing. If you reward your 10-pound puppy's jumping on you with kisses or treats, you probably realize by now that your actions are reinforcing the dog's bad behavior and it won't be so appealing when he grows to 100 pounds. If it isn't already too late, start training your young dog that jumping on people is not acceptable behavior, as retraining is time-consuming, confusing for your dog, and can be difficult.

Your dog's tendency to jump on people is more than an inconvenient annoyance; it's dangerous. Even a smaller dog can knock a human off balance, especially a child or older adult. Not only does your poorly trained dog embarrass you and pose a threat to others – but it also puts you at risk of being targeted in a lawsuit.

To train your puppy not to jump, whenever the dog jumps on you or someone else, you should gently put his feet back down on the floor. Once all four of his feet are on the floor – and remain there – load on the praise! For the sake of your puppy's training, ask everyone in the family to follow this procedure if the puppy jumps on them. You can even ask guests to get with the program! Because if you don't accept this behavior, but the puppy's impression is that others do, he'll be confused about what appropriate behavior is regarding jumping on people. Consistency is definitely a plus when it comes to dog training – consistency not just from you, but from others in the family.

Straining and Pulling at the Leash

Your puppy is probably enthusiastic and eager – one of the things we love about them is their unflagging zest for life. But his enthusiasm can sometimes result in him being overly eager and pulling on the leash.

Your first goal is not to initiate or encourage pulling on the leash by playing tug-of-war with your puppy with the leash, or anything that resembles a leash, like a length of rope. Instead, choose a toy in the shape of a ring if you want to play tug-of-war with him.

If your puppy pulls and you are having trouble training him not to, consider using a body harness. For the process of getting him to accept the body harness, refer back to the process described in Chapter 4 of getting your puppy to accept a collar and leash. When choosing a harness, try it on your dog before purchasing; some dogs have a particular body type that may make finding a harness that fits a challenge; for example, corgis can be particularly long from ears to shoulders, making it hard to fit them in a harness.

Practice good habits when walking your dog, encouraging him to keep his head level with your knee and to walk by your side. A well-fitted training collar or choke chain can help your dog understand just where you want his head to be.

Don't continuously pull back on the leash when your puppy pulls ahead. Instead, quickly change directions to make your puppy suddenly fall behind you. Anticipate the puppy and change directions before he reaches the end of the leash, or you could put too much pressure on his neck when your direction changes. Keep the leash loose except for that moment when your direction changes – you should feel a slight tug on the leash, and then loosen it immediately.

Never pull or yank the puppy's neck to correct him. You should apply steady pressure, gently, rather than a hard yank. Aim to use the least amount of pressure possible to get your puppy headed in the right direction, in the correct position.

Just as you don't want to play tug-of-war with the leash, don't let your puppy pull on the leash and pull you around. Consistency in how you use the leash – what it is and is not for – is essential to teaching the dog how to use it properly. If you have a dog that is going to be very large, take particular advantage of his smaller puppy-years to train him to the leash, because it will be a lot easier now than when he weighs 150 pounds.

Escaping and Roaming

Can you imagine letting your dog out the front door to roam up and down the street, and from yard to yard? Just the thought of what could happen probably takes your breath away – the dangers from cars, encounters with other animals, adventures with open garbage cans and other possible incidents probably make your imagination run wild.

It is illegal in most towns for dogs to roam free, and a roaming dog is likely to be picked up by animal control - which is almost certain to be unpleasant, expensive and dangerous for your dog.

But if the thought of your dog roaming free scares the dickens out of you, it's a pretty sure bet your dog sees it differently. Outside your fence or out your front door are an array of scents and sounds that most dogs are just dying to investigate further, and if your dog can escape your yard or your house – and you haven't trained him not to – he almost certainly will.

Preventing his escape is much easier – and much safer – than it is to try to recapture a dog that's gotten loose. So here are some precautions and preventative measures you can take, ahead of time, to keep your dog on your premises.

First, do what you can to keep your dog engaged where he is – if he's bored, he's much more likely to investigate ways to get out and entertain himself. So surround him with all the things he might need – a warm, soft bed, a filled water bowl and plenty of toys, and your dog will likely spend some time playing, take a nice long drink of water, and flop over in his bed to rest and dream – safe and sound.

It's also a really good approach to exercise your dog regularly, to use up all that energy he might otherwise use to escape. Especially for an energetic dog or a very intelligent one that gets bored easily, schedule lots of high-energy play sessions several times a day, and at least one good, long walk. It's especially good to wear the dog out right before you leave the house. Again – he's likely, then, to just seek out his bed and sleep till you return.

Next, address your house and fence and make sure you've done all you can to make it escape-proof. If your dog digs, you may need to extend the fence a few inches into the ground. If he jumps, your fence will need to be higher. If a deeper fence or a higher one are not enough to keep him in, you may need to never let him outside without supervision, and confine him to the inside of the house, if you aren't going to be at home. Do whatever you need to do to ensure he doesn't get out to roam because a roaming dog is in danger and the result could truly be heartbreaking.

Chapter 9: Advanced Dog Training Exercises

If your dog has mastered the basic training, congratulations! You are a good and responsible dog owner, and deserve to be the head of your dog's pack, because you're taking your responsibility seriously and putting in the time and effort to look out for his well-being.

The basic commands probably give you everything you need for your dog to be an enjoyable companion dog, but if you and he enjoyed the training, and want to continue, following are some advanced skills you can train for.

Before you begin, make sure your dog is unwaveringly strong with the "come when called" command. It is the basis for most advanced training. If your dog is not absolutely solid with this command, your training should not begin until he is. Return to the guidelines in Chapter 7 for training to come when called.

When you're ready to begin advanced training, motivate your dog – and yourself – by making the training fun. Because training involves consistency and repetition, it can become boring. Shake it up a bit by choosing a variety of locations for your training, use different toys to motivate your dog, and perhaps bookend the training with different ways of playing or different activities. Keep it interesting for both of you.

If your training is based on rewards with food, be sure your dog is motivated by the treat. Dog owners may swear to the effectiveness of this treat or that, but different dogs like different things. You don't want to get all the way out to a park to train, only to find the treat you brought with you doesn't motivate your dog at all. Start with healthier treats and see if they motivate your dog – a bit of apple, or lean meat, or a bit of his regular food. If needed, go to the less healthy but tasty treats, such as liver or an appealing store-bought treat. Be aware of the foods you should never use to treat your dog, such as chocolate or raisins.

Get the treats ready ahead of time. Cut them into small pieces, about a quarter of an inch or smaller. Using small pieces lets you give him treats a number of times without overfeeding him.

Games to Play in Advanced Training

A game that's fun for you, your dog, or another family member or friend is just calling the dog back and forth. This is a great exercise to use to teach the dog to come when called, not just to you, but to others in the family. All the training you've done with your dog has created the bond and the relationship you wanted, but it's important he also responds to other members of the family, or friends that might dog-sit for you from time to time. He needs to know to respond to whatever person is in charge if you aren't around.

Back-and-forth is simple and fun. Use two people or more, each standing about 10 yards from each other in a safe environment, like a fenced backyard. The first person calls the dog, and when he comes, he gets a treat and is commanded to sit and stay (it's important that the person who called is the person who gives the dog the treat). The dog should remain in the stay until the next person calls him, and he goes, gets a treat, and is put in the sit/stay again. Dogs love this game.

Once your dog gets the idea of back-and-forth, try hide-and-seek. For this game, two or more people start in the center of the house. The first person calls the dog to come, gives him a treat, and puts him in sit/stay. The second person moves across the room and does the same. As that person rewards the dog, the other person moves out into the house, hiding, so that when they call to the dog, he has to find them. Meanwhile, the other person is finding a place to hide. This is a wonderful game because your dog's natural instincts are probably to seek out food using sounds and scents.

Keeping it Fun and Engaging

Keeping your dog's attention during training requires some effort and imagination. Your dog is probably easily distracted, so keeping it interesting is not just motivating – it's also a way to keep the dog safe, by keeping his attention on you and the activity. Additionally, making the training fun creates a stronger bond with the dog, gives him confidence, and makes training go faster.

Don't fall into a routine. Walk in different areas. Go for rides in the car. Set up play dates with other dogs. Vary the toys you use. Do whatever you can to hold his attention, and to reward him in a variety of ways for all his successes, big or small. Remember the power of the reward, whether that's a special treat or a scratch in his favorite spot. Let your dog realize that every time he obeys you and shows approved behavior, something good will happen, and he'll be motivated to please you each and every time.

Distraction Training

You are seldom in an environment with your dog that you can control completely; even when training in the house, a passing siren, bike rider or jogger can pull your dog's attention to the outside, and away from you. Do your best not to let distractions disrupt your training. Teach your dog to ignore distractions of any kind, and keep his focus on you, for the sake of his training and his safety.

You can teach your dog to ignore distraction by providing a distraction and asking him to turn away from it and re-focus on you. Here's an exercise: if your dog enjoys socializing with other dogs, let him play in a neighbor's yard, running free with another dog. Then call him to you. When he comes, you know the routine — lots of enthusiastic praise, and perhaps a treat for a reward. Then immediately allow him to return to playing. Repeat, rewarding him each time and releasing him again immediately. He'll quickly learn that he can come to you when called, be rewarded, and then get to return to what he likes.

This is advanced training because it likely goes against your dog's nature. Most dogs are easily distracted, and they can bring an intense focus to what they're enthused about and that makes it hard for you to pull their focus away, and back to you. So if your dog doesn't get the hang of distraction training right away, don't let it discourage you. Handlers acknowledge this is one of the most difficult trainings for your dog to master.

Be creative in getting the dog to come to you, especially if you're having trouble getting him to obey. Try waving his favorite toy to get his attention. If you've trained your dog using clicker training, you can use a click as the needed motivation and focal point.

Once your dog is responding well and switching his focus over to you, you should drop the visual cues or clicker cues, and get the dog to respond when you only use your voice to call him to you. You can probably imagine why; if you find yourself in a situation without a toy or a clicker at hand, you still need to ensure the dog will respond, and respond immediately.

Whatever it takes, it is important to keep at it until your dog can turn his focus to you, and what you want, in every situation. There will come a time when getting your dog to refocus on you and come if he's distracted is essential for his safety and the safety of others. Do whatever you need to do to prepare for that day so that your dog responds well, and you retain control.

Chapter 10: House and Crate Training

For your dog to be a companion that you can enjoy, it's essential he be well housetrained. The number one reason dogs are surrendered to an animal shelter is that they are not house trained. As with other approaches to training in this book, the approach we suggest involves using the dog's nature, his instincts and natural tendencies, to make training easy and intuitive.

Dogs are instinctively clean animals, and that's the quality that can make house training easier. You would rather your dog not soil the areas where you live, and where he sleeps and eats. Great news: he would rather not soil those areas either!

Training is also made easier by the dog's tendency to develop the habit of urinating or defecating in specific spots and on particular surfaces; for example, if your dog becomes used to eliminating on concrete, he'll seek out that surface in preference to eliminating on grass, dirt – or carpet. The approach to training that follows makes the most of your dog's natural tendency to keep his living area clean and to eliminate on a particular surface.

There are two approaches we suggest – house training, which is a better approach for larger dogs, and crate training, which is generally a better approach for small dogs and puppies. Choose the approach that best fits you and your dog.

House Training

Both house training and crate training are based on confining the dog to a specified space. With house training, that area is his "den," or training area. With crate training, the dog is confined to his crate. Let's begin by going over the recommended approaches to house training your dog.

Setting Up the Training Area

The first step in house training your dog is to set up your training area. A small, confined space such as a bathroom, or part of a kitchen or garage, works best as a training area. Choose an area that you will want to spend some time in because it's important for you to keep your dog company in the training area. You'll want to play with your dog there, and the dog will eat and sleep there. Set a bed up for him in the chosen area – anything from a bed bought online or from a pet store, to a towel or towels you put in a large box for him. Don't be discouraged if the dog eliminates in this area at first; once he recognizes that this is his space, his natural tendencies will keep him from soiling it.

Later, when your dog has gotten used to his bed, you can move it to other areas of the house. For now, when you aren't going to be with your dog, he should be confined to the area you've chosen as his training area.

Setting Up the Toilet Area

You've chosen a training area; now choose your dog's toilet area. Choose an area that:

- will always be available to your puppy when he needs to eliminate.

- has a surface, such as gravel or concrete, that is unlike any surface anywhere in your house. This ensures the puppy understands he is never to eliminate in the house.

In the early days of training, it's important for you to be with the dog each time he goes to the toilet area until he develops the habit of eliminating there. Your presence will help ensure he only uses the area you've established as his toilet area.

To make training easier and more predictable, settle on a feeding schedule, and stick to it. That way, his elimination habits will also be regular. If you can predict when your dog will need to eliminate, you can make sure you're available to accompany him, and guide him in using the area you've chosen – and nowhere else.

Your first goal is to get the dog to use the toilet area regularly and to take him there, in case he needs to eliminate, several times a day. Once that routine is established, never confine the dog to his training area without giving him access to his toilet area. If he is unable to wait to eliminate and eliminates in his training area, it can set your house training back.

Continuing the House Training Process

With consistency and praise, your dog will soon only eliminate in the toilet area, and never in the training area. Now it's time to extend his training to the rest of the house. Take your time with this phase of the training. Start by adding one room; when he is completely able to control his bladder and bowels in that room, you can extend the area to another room. Again – do not rush this process. It's better to take all the time you need to ensure the dog can control his elimination process with one additional room than it is to move too fast and have to back up and re-train because the dog wasn't ready.

When you are ready to expand to a room beyond the training area, you should let the dog play, eat and sleep in the new room – but only when you are there to supervise. When you are not with your dog, he should only be left alone in the training area.

In time, the dog will recognize the new room is an extension of the training area, and you can add another room, and so on, until the dog can be relied on to control elimination in any area of the house.

Take all the time your dog needs to move through these steps; it's easier to take your time now than retrain for problems later. As with other training, use every opportunity to praise him enthusiastically when he uses the established area for elimination. Don't punish him for mistakes; that will only confuse him, and slow the training process down.

The Do's and Don'ts of House Training

Set aside the time needed to work with your puppy to establish proper toilet habits. The work you do with him now will ensure he's an enjoyable companion for years to come — or, if your training is spotty or rushed, it will ensure he is not. Give this training what it needs to be thorough and successful.

It's best to wait until your puppy is six months old to train him. Younger puppies aren't able to control their bowel and bladder; to attempt training is to risk them feeling confused, shamed and in all ways negative around house training, and you don't want that.

Until your puppy is six months old, confine him to a room that's small and easily puppy-proofed. Cover the floor with newspaper or some other absorbent material, and be sure you change the paper every time it gets soiled. In the beginning, this can be a pretty demanding process, but as the puppy grows and uses a toilet area, you'll use less and less paper.

The Do's of House Training Your Puppy

- Your puppy should always be able to access his toilet area. To get him in the habit of using it when you're home with him, take him to his toilet area at least every 45 minutes.

- If you can't be home or are busy with something and can't supervise your dog, put him in his puppy-proofed room lined with paper and free of anything he might chew on or eat. That way, he won't soil his training area.

- The puppy's toilet area should be a surface that is unlike any floor in your home. Possibilities are concrete, asphalt, grass or dirt. Do not choose a toilet area surface that in any way resembles hardwood floors, carpet or tile.

- You should praise your puppy and reward him when he uses the toilet area to eliminate. Your puppy needs to associate using the toilet area with things that are positive and that make him happy – toys, treats and lots of enthusiastic praise.

- Keep your puppy on a feeding schedule, and give him plenty of clean, fresh water to drink. That way, you can better predict when he'll need to go to his toilet area, and you can plan to accompany him.

- Consider using a crate for housetraining your puppy. Information on how to crate train follows in this chapter.

- Above all, remember to be patient throughout the process of housetraining your dog. Give it all the time it takes — and it could take several months. That may seem like a long time, but you are training your dog to be a companion to you and your family for years to come. Best to train him right the first time.

The Don'ts of House Training Your Puppy:

- Never lose your patience or your temper with your puppy over mistakes. Remember — punishing him will just confuse him, and cause him to be fearful. It will set your training back.

- Don't leave food out for your puppy to eat all day or all night. Establish a feeding schedule, and pick up any uneaten food. That way you can better predict your puppy's toilet schedule.

- Go from training area to one additional room, and then another, and take your time. Do not let your puppy have free access to the rest of the house until you've thoroughly trained him.

Your Dog's Particular Needs

House training any dog is challenging, and some dogs are particularly challenging to train. However your dog takes to the training, it is your job as his pack leader to be patient, loving, generous and consistent with him. If you lose your temper or your patience or shame your dog, he will become frightened and lose his confidence, and that will do serious damage to your training and your relationship with him.

Your dog may present particular challenges and needs around house training; it's important to pay attention to him, and the signals he's sending.

Expect some slip-ups. When accidents happen, stay calm and positive. Accidents may be an indication that you're moving too fast with the training; or, they can indicate the dog needs more time with you in his training area and accompanying him to his toilet area. If accidents are happening too frequently, let yourself take a step back in the training and begin again.

Though it may seem odd to give a dog treats in his toilet area, it's important to reward him in several ways – toys, treats and praise – when he eliminates there. He needs to associate the toilet area with positive things. If you find it unpleasant to be there, just give it the few extra moments it takes to praise him and reward him so training will go well.

To keep from challenging the puppy too much, keep his training area small. As he learns to use the toilet area and is showing signs of being reliable, you can expand his training area. Just don't make the area too large too quickly. Its size needs to be expanded slowly.

As with the leash and collar, some dogs don't respond well to the training area at first. If your dog is used to the outdoors and has never been confined, he may act as though his training is a prison, and bark or cry or whine and try to get out. Give him time, just as you may have had to do with leash and collar; in time, he'll learn his training area is a safe place for him, and not something meant to imprison him.

One problem you may encounter with your dog around house training is boredom. If your dog is bored (and particularly intelligent breeds like Siberian Huskies may become bored easily), he may drink much more water during the day. Greater intake of water results in a need to urinate much more often, increasing the likelihood that he will urinate in his training area (which you never want to happen). It is his nature and instinct to keep the area where he lives clean, so being unable to control urinating in his training area can make him confused and frightened. That can set your house training efforts back.

How to prevent your dog from becoming bored? Toys are a great approach. Give him a variety to choose from, and take some time to play with him, showing him how the toys can be used, and piquing his interest in them. Then leave them in a place in his training area that's easily accessible for him, so he can choose various toys throughout the day.

Also give him a designated place to sleep, with a comfy dog bed, or a large box he can easily get in and out of, and cushioned with towels. Give him lots of exercise and play time, so he'll sleep while you're away from home.

Dealing with House Training Issues

Dogs are generally clean animals whose nature is to avoid using his living area as a toilet. Your dog's instinct is to keep his sleeping area free of any soiling or urination. You can use those instincts to make training easier. That's the approach taken with both crate training (which confines the dog to his crate when you are away) and house training (which confines the dog to a small room or other area in the home).

This training approach works well for both puppies and older dogs. If you're experiencing problems with house training, it's likely the result of missing the signals your dog is sending you, being less than consistent with feeding, or trying to move too fast in the training.

Here are some pointers on what to look into and what to change if your house training isn't going the way you'd like.

- Don't try to speed up the training process. You'll see the quickest results by being consistent with feeding, keeping to a schedule to take the dog out (every 45 minutes is a good approach), and lavishing praise for good behavior and obedience. If you truly want a well-trained dog in the shortest amount of time, take the time you need to train him well the first time. In the long run, you'll get there sooner by taking things more slowly.

- If your dog continues to soil his training area, the most likely explanation is that he's been left there too long. Take him out to eliminate every 45 minutes when you're home. Give him play time outside his training area. Also, consider that the training area – his den – is too large. Use a screen or other blocking to make it smaller, or move him to a smaller room, such as the laundry room. Even if you do arrange for him to be in a smaller area, continue to take him out frequently to give him a chance to eliminate.

- If your dog is soiling his bed, it's again likely that you've left him there for too long without a chance to eliminate, and the dog has been unable to avoid having an accident. Another possible explanation is that the dog may not have realized the area is, indeed, his bed – signs that this is the issue would be that he's sleeping somewhere else in the training area.

- If your dog shows signs of anxiety when you put him in his training area, or whines, chews or barks incessantly, he may not feel safe and secure in his training area, or may think of it as being caged. Spend time with him in the training area, playing and being affectionate. Praise him when you take him to the area and he behaves well. In time, having the area as a safe place to sleep and eat should help him welcome it as a place that is his "den."

- While guides such as this book are a big help in house training, never forget to be observant of your dog and his particular needs and characteristics. Your dog wants to keep his living area clean. If he is not, observe him and use some creative thinking to try to understand what his issues are.

- If you've tried a number of solutions and different approaches, have a vet check your dog for a UTI or other medical condition that might be the cause.

House training is not an easy process, or a quick one, but your success at this training will lead to you having a dog that can roam freely through the house, and be with you where you are, whether you're reading the paper, or watching television – without soiling the house where he lives, and you do too.

Crate Training for Dogs and Puppies

Both house training and crate training are based on confining the dog to a specified space. With house training, that area is his "den," or training area. With crate training, the dog is confined to his crate.

Many dog experts agree that crate training is a particularly effective way to housebreak dogs, whether your dog is a puppy or full-grown. As with house training, crate training works so well because it is based on your dog's instinctual desire to keep his living area clean.

With crate training, the dog is frequently placed in the crate and it becomes his "den," his living space; it's natural for him to avoid soiling the area where he eats and sleeps. Placing the dog in his crate uses this instinct to teach him not to soil there.

Tips for Crate Training

- As with house training, crate training is more successful if you establish a routine. The dog's routine, followed faithfully, will greatly enhance his ability to only eliminate in the designated place. Establish his toilet area; then praise him and reward him every time he eliminates there. Your response should only be praise; if he has an accident in a place other than his designated toilet area, do not express anger or frustration, or you'll set his crate training back.

- You will need to confine your dog to his crate whenever you are out of the house, or he will be unsupervised. That way, he'll think of the crate as his den, or his home, and follow his natural instincts not to soil his home.

- If you choose crate training as your method of training your dog, be sure to always remove him from the crate as soon as possible when you return home. Immediately take him to the established toilet area. This is an opportunity to give positive reinforcement; he'll almost certainly need to urinate or defecate. When he does so in the designated area, give praise and reward him with a toy or a treat. That way, he'll associate using his toilet area – rather than any other area – with good things, such as your attention, your praise, and treats or toys.

- Never leave your dog in his crate for too long a period of time. If you do, and he's forced to soil his living area, he'll be confused, frightened and shamed. That could set your training program back by several weeks.

- If you confine your dog to his crate while you are at home, give him an opportunity to relieve himself every 45 minutes. The procedure is to take him out of his crate, immediately put his collar and leash on him, and take him outside to his toilet area. There, give him five minutes to do his business. If he doesn't eliminate during that time period, return him to his crate. And if he does, of course you should reward him with praise, a treat, playtime, a walk, or in any way that gives him a positive impression of his behavior.

- It's recommended that you keep a diary of when your dog urinates or defecates. Compare that to the time at which he was fed, and other events around the house (you're coming home, another family member coming home, etc.). Your goal is to get a good idea of what time or what events create his need to eliminate, and that will give you good insight during this training process.

If you are patient and thorough in your crate training, in time you'll be able to let your dog move about the house freely, a companion there by your side, ready to be enjoyed at any time.

Dealing with Accidents during Crate Training

For your crate training to be successful, and be completed in as short a time as possible, it's essential that you never get angry or punish your puppy or dog if he has an accident or makes a mistake. Don't react or respond to an accident. Instead, just clean it up.

If you find yourself frustrated or angry when your dog has an accident, consider that the accident probably wouldn't have happened if you had taken a different approach to the training, giving it more of your time and effort, praising more often, or being patient with the process.

Of course, you look forward to the day your dog can have free access to every part of the house; but to rush that is to risk the dog having an accident, which will throw him into a range of difficult feelings, fear, and shame. So do not give your dog access to unsupervised time in your home until you are sure you can rely on his bladder and bowel to only soil using the toilet area. If an accident does happen, return to crate training. As hard as it may be, realize that repeating a few steps of the training will mean you can give your dog free access throughout your home sooner, and with complete confidence.

Chapter 11: Training for Behavior Issues

Your dog may be one of those loving, sweet, calm and well-adjusted companions that takes to training easily and without challenges. But more often, dogs will show certain tendencies toward bad or challenging behavior – chewing, biting, barking, or being fearful of noises or new situations. In particular, as more and more generous people adopt rescue dogs, they may find themselves dealing with bad behaviors engendered by their dog's past. Here are some common behaviors, and how to establish a relationship and focus on training to help your dog get past his challenges.

Building Confidence and Respect

Before you can hope to have success with any training – but especially, with training for challenging behaviors – the first thing you must do is win your dog's respect, and give him reason to trust and have confidence in you. You have his nature as a pack animal to help you – your dog wants a leader he can trust and follow. It makes him feel safe and secure. He has a natural instinct, and a natural need, to submit to a strong leader. So your first goal as a trainer is to build or reinforce your dog's perception of you as that leadership figure.

If you don't yet have the respect and trust of your dog, it's likely your training will be difficult at best, and possibly unsuccessful. If you don't have the relationship with your dog that you need to have, give it the time it takes to develop – however much time that is. Some dogs give trust and respect easily, but with others, it has to be earned. The way to do that is through experiences that give your dog a positive interaction with you. Once you win that trust and respect, you'll be amazed at the difference it makes in your training efforts.

"I'm fine," you might think, "I know my dog adores me!" That's great, but it's not always the same thing as having your dog's trust and respect. Your puppy may give you lots of love and affirmation that you're the center of his world, but that may be because you let him get away with bad behavior (because it's cute when they are small!), or you let him take advantage of you. That doesn't mean you have a bad dog – without the guidance of a strong pack leader, a dog is going to go his own way. As his trainer and owner, your job is to find a balance between love and affection, and the kind of respect that your dog would naturally give its pack leader. That kind of respect comes from setting clear boundaries and conveying what is and is not acceptable, and it sets the stage for productive training.

It's in your dog's nature to appreciate the strength and leadership you show, and the boundaries you set. The pack mentality is that a strong pack leader (that would be you) protects and guides the pack. In a pack with a strong leader, every dog knows his own place, what is expected of him, and how to succeed. It's a dynamic that allows the pack to function as a single entity – something that strong training will allow you to achieve with your dog. In actuality, your dog longs for this type of leadership. It makes him feel safe and secure; without it, he may lack confidence and struggle with feelings of fear and confusion.

If you don't win the respect of your dog, you won't only be making him, and probably yourself, unhappy; you are actually putting yourself and your dog in danger. Unless your dog respects you, he can be hard to live with at best, and dangerous to you, himself and others at worst. So do yourself and your dog a favor; be that strong pack leader that he needs, establishing firm boundaries and clear expectations, consistently. If you're worried about including enough love and affection in your relationship, rest assured that the basis for the training in this book is praise and reward. You'll be giving your dog plenty of time, attention and positive reinforcement – but within the context of good boundaries.

If you have a puppy and are giving it the time it needs for training and socialization, trust and respect will naturally follow. Don't put training and socialization off – it's important to start gaining your puppy's respect and trust when he's still very young. That also gives you the opportunity to establish a strong bond with him from the get-go.

Remember he's just a puppy, with a short attention span, so keep your first few training sessions very short. You don't want to wear him out or bore him – he should finish the session still wanting more. Even older dogs are generally unable to focus beyond 15 minutes of training. Make your lessons shorter, so you can leave your dog with a positive experience rather than a negative one.

Another way to bring a positive note to training is to always start the session with play, and end it with play as well. Dogs are quick to make associations between one thing and another; if your sessions are short, and begin and end with play, your dog will associate training as a fun time when he gets to be with you and has your full attention. Add to that plenty of praise and positive reinforcement for your dog's good behavior, and your dog will be a happy dog, willing to please and easy to train.

Guard against boredom. Basic skills such as sit/stay and heeling are important, but a little dry. You shouldn't go from one command to the next. Instead, mix it up – include some fun in between basic training. It will give your dog a break, and give you one too.

With a solid grounding in mutual respect and trust, you and your dog will not only be able to train well; you'll have laid the groundwork you need should you need to deal with particular challenges, like the ones that follow.

Dealing with Separation Anxiety

"Separation anxiety" or "owner absent misbehavior" is a behavior challenge that dog trainers see a great deal. It can manifest in a number of ways – the destruction of furniture and other property, compulsive chewing, uncontrolled urination and defecation, excessive barking, and more.

If your dog suffers from separation anxiety, he is not a happy dog. He may whine, cry, bark, dig, howl, chew and scratch at the doors and walls whenever you're away. It may be your instinct to stay home more with the dog; but remember, the goal of training is to teach the dog to adjust to what you need, not the other way around. For your relationship with your dog to be a healthy and enjoyable one, your dog needs to be able to handle being separated from you for extended periods of time.

If your dog is dealing with separation anxiety, here are some ways to help mitigate his anxiety.

- Be aware that the way in which you leave the house has an effect on your dog's separation anxiety issues. When you're ready to leave – leave. A long, emotional, drawn-out goodbye raises your dog's anxiety level before you even get out the door, and makes your dog feel even lonelier once you're gone. Such intense attention can excite him; then suddenly the door closes, he's alone, and has no way to let that excess energy go. So he finds ways to release that energy and anxiety through destructive behavior, chewing at the rug or furniture, or ripping up sofa cushions.

- Consider that your dog may be responding to excess energy, rather than separation anxiety. The coping behaviors can be very much the same, but actually, excess energy is much more easily addressed. Simply giving the dog more exercise will give him a better balance of activity and excitement, combined with periods of quiet and rest. See if just exercising more eliminates his bad behavior.

- If you do determine that your dog is suffering from separation anxiety, you'll need to figure out the root cause of his response to help him change his behavior. Your dog will experience less anxiety if he is happy, secure, safe and comfortable, both when you are at home and when you are away. Give your dog what he needs – healthy food, good fresh water, toys to hold his interest, exercise, and plenty of time with you, whether that's to train or just to play together. Give him things to hold his interest when you're away – balls, toys and chew toys. Consider that your dog is a pack animal, and needs others in his pack; that's a big part of his anxiety when you are away. His pack is incomplete, as a single dog does not make a pack. So getting another animal, such as another dog or a cat, can give your dog the feeling of "pack" that he needs, and also give him a playmate so he can have fun and keep occupied when you're away.

- Giving your dog enough exercise and play time with you – giving him your undivided attention – helps alleviate separation anxiety and the boredom that can cause it. It lets your dog be active in a way that will make him more likely just to sleep when you are away, and become active again on your return. So schedule at least one play sessions each day, preferably before you leave the house. Try to schedule it so that it ends at least thirty minutes before you leave, so the dog will have a chance to settle down and be more likely to lay down for a nap, as soon as you leave.

- If your dog is experiencing anxiety when you leave and are gone and is behaving in ways that are a problem, such as destructive chewing or incessant barking, try to get him accustomed to your being gone. Try leaving for short periods of time, and then returning, several times a day; that gets him used to the idea that, if he's uncomfortable with you leaving, it won't be for long, and you're certainly not leaving him forever. This is especially important with dogs that have been abandoned at shelters, or who have been lost and on their own. Helping your dog realize that when you leave it isn't permanent will go a long way toward decreasing his anxiety.

Teaching your Dog Not to Chase

If your dog is prone to chasing, that's a throwback to his genetic history as a predatory animal. All predators have the impulse to chase what is fleeing – it's the same reason your dog enjoys chasing a ball. But just because he's acting out of a natural instinct, that doesn't make chasing a good thing, or something you have to live with. Certainly, joggers, mailmen, and people on bicycles would appreciate it if you worked with your dog to rid him of this behavior.

Chasing may seem like a minor nuisance when your dog is young and small. It's quite another matter when he's grown to be a big, heavy dog that can pose a serious threat. It's important to train your dog not to chase people for any reason, and as with other training, it's best if you can start that training when the dog is very young.

Training Your Dog Not to Chase Others

You should not let your dog off the leash until you know he

doesn't chase, or until you've trained him not to. Letting him chase is dangerous to him and to others. It's irresponsible of you as an owner, is illegal, and could leave you in a position in which you are liable for being sued.

So train your dog in a controlled area, like a fenced-in yard, and make sure he isn't prone to chasing before you risk him getting free. If he is prone to chasing, you'll need to choose training areas where he won't be distracted by people or animals he'd like to chase. You need him to focus when you are training him, so he can more quickly understand the behavior you want from him. You will be asking him to perform commands over and over again to reach a place where he responds in the correct way, automatically. A distraction – such as something his instinct tells him to chase – pulls his focus away, and slows the training down.

So hold any training sessions away from the temptation to chase, but in particular, hold training about not chasing indoors, in your home, to ensure he won't be distracted. Put him on leash and stand with him at the end of a hallway, or the edge of a room. Wave a tennis ball in front of your dog, but don't let him touch the ball. Then, roll the ball across the room, or to the end of the hallway, giving the command "Off" to tell your dog he is not to chase after the ball. If he starts to go after the ball, give him the command "Off" once again, and tug the leash firmly.

During this training, make certain your dog does not touch the ball. If he reaches it, he may be confused into thinking that the "Off" command means "Go get the ball!" By repeating this exercise a number of times, your dog will learn what you mean by the "Off" command. Of course, when your dog figures it out and responds in the way you want by not chasing down the ball, praise him to the skies and reward him with a special treat.

At that point, repeat the exercise a few times to make absolutely certain your dog understands, praising each time he performs well. Then move to another area of the house and do the exercise again. When your dog obeys the "Off" command in several areas of your house, try the same exercise off-leash – but still only work with him while inside your house, or from within a fenced-in yard. Give your dog all the time he needs to learn not to chase; the instinct to chase may be strong in him, and rushing the process will only slow his learning down in the long run. It's also important not to rush the training because to do so is to take the risk he'll chase another animal or a person, and not have been trained in a way that gives you any control over him.

When you think he's fully ready, test your dog's ability to resist chasing out in the "real" world. To test him, get help from a friend who is willing to pose as a jogger. It's better if the friend is someone your dog has never seen before – he needs to believe this "jogger" is a stranger. Stand near the street, holding your dog on a leash. When the friend comes jogging by, give the "Off" command. Your dog should not move toward the jogger in any way. If he does, firmly tug on the leash; if he performs well, praise and reward him.

Training Your Dog Not to Chase Cars

If your dog chases people or other dogs, he is more likely a threat to them than they are to him. But if he chases cars, he is the one most likely to be hurt, possibly fatally. As early as possible in his life, train your dog to understand that chasing cars is never, ever acceptable. A dog that chases a car may one day be a dog that catches a car, and nothing good will come of that.

Dogs chase cars for a number of reasons. First, there's the hunting instinct to chase what moves. That's an ingrained behavior, instinctual to some dogs, particularly those from hunting or herding breeds, like your new Siberian Husky puppy. A dog that's from a breed bred for hunting experiences a thrill when he engages in a chase. A herding dog is instinctively trying to control which direction a moving car moves in, but just because the behavior is instinctual, that doesn't make it desirable in any way. Much of the training you've done with your dog has been to work with him to overcome his instinctual response, and this training is no exception. Understand that he is responding based on instinct, and he isn't deliberately disobeying you when he chases a car; but even so, it's important that you train him to obey your commands.

Your dog may be drawn to chase cars not out of defensiveness, but out of joy; many dogs associate cars with fun trips with you. Most dogs love to ride in the car, and some dog behaviorists believe they chase cars hoping to get a ride.

But it doesn't matter why your dog chases cars, because whatever his reason, it's imperative that you put a stop to this dangerous activity as soon as you can. The "Off" command that was covered earlier is the basis of training your dog not to chase cars. It's a powerful command with a number of uses and should be thoroughly understood and obeyed by every dog.

With the "Off" command, you are instructing your dog to stay where he is – no matter how interested or excited he is by a passing dog, jogger, bicyclist or car. Training your dog not to chase cars involves "distraction training."

For this training, put your dog's leash and collar on him. You'll need the help of at least one other person (the "distraction"). This training volunteer will slowly drive by, in front of your dog, luring him into a chase. It's really best if the volunteer drives your car, as dogs can distinguish one car from another, and yours is particularly appealing – especially if that's the car your dog is used to being in when he goes for rides.

As your friend drives by, watch carefully to see how your dog reacts. If he moves at all, whether a small movement or a jump or lunge, give the "Off" command and immediately return him to the sitting position. If he stays put, let him know he did exactly what you wanted by praising him and giving him something tasty.

Repeat this training several times over the course of the next several days. As your dog begins to obey you, move to the next level of the training by standing further away from your dog for the test. You can easily accomplish this with a retractable leash, lengthened to put your dog further away from you. At each stage, when your dog is fully obeying the "Off" command, lengthen the distance more, but always make sure you retain control.

You may think the goal of this training is to allow you to have your dog outside, off-leash, safely, but your dog is never entirely safe if he is outside and off-leash. The training to prevent him from chasing cars, other animals, or people is just to give you an extra measure of safety, in case you ever have him outside and off-leash – which, again, you should never do. Always have him on his leash, or supervised, or, best of all, both. Remember – dogs can be unpredictable, especially when tempted. Ensure your dog is trained in the "Off" command, in case his chase instinct kicks in and you need to get control of him so he and others are safe.

Socializing and Training the Shy or Fearful Dog

You probably work with and know people who are outgoing; and others who are more shy and withdrawn. It's the same with dogs – some puppies are confident and bold, and always will be, while they may have a sibling that is shy and more hesitant. You can watch them play and easily tell which is which. A shyer dog will hold back, standing at the edge of the group of dogs, fearful of the older, stronger dogs and the roughhousing. Other puppies are always in the thick of things, jostling to get control, romping and wrestling with siblings, often whether the sibling wants to or not.

As with much of the training discussed in this book, it's important to know your dog and adjust training to suit his nature, when adjusting it is possible. If you are working with a strong-willed, confident and forceful dog, that presents particular challenges to you as the trainer. If you are working with a dog or puppy that is shy or fearful, you have very different challenges.

One challenge to owning a dog that is shy and fearful is that they are more likely to bite. That may seem counter-intuitive – you may think a confident, forceful dog would be more likely to bite, and indeed, not all aggression is based on a dog's fear. But a shy dog that is fearful is likely to become a biter to deal with that fear, particularly in an unfamiliar situation. That response can be dangerous — for you, for your dog, and for others. So it's important to teach a shy dog, whatever its age, to be confident, and to know that new situations and new people are nothing he should fear.

How do you know if your dog is fearful? You can tell he is if he is afraid of strangers, uneasy and unsettled in new situations, and prone to avoid certain people, or certain objects, such as a broom. You may also be able to tell he's fearful if you've noticed he has a tendency to bite, particularly when he feels cornered.

If you recognize your dog or puppy is fearful, act immediately. Fear responses in a dog can quickly become ingrained — and once they are, they are very difficult to shift or erase. This is one of the reasons this book stresses socializing your puppy because a socialized young puppy is much less likely to be fearful and much less likely to become a dog that bites out of fear. If you take your puppy from his litter at a young age and he is the only dog in your house, make sure he has plenty of opportunities to play with other dogs and other puppies. Your goal here is to put your puppy into new situations and let him learn to adapt. That will give him confidence, and help him adjust to new situations when he is grown.

One note: it's vital that the socialization you provide for your puppy is always positive. One bad experience can instill fear in him that it may take months to overcome. In particular, make sure any adult dog or other animal he interacts with is gentle, well-adjusted and sociable. It's fine for an adult dog to gently teach your puppy that his play biting is too rough; you just want to be sure you avoid situations in which the older dog or other animal completely dominates your puppy in a threatening way or becomes overly aggressive and violent with him.

You want to be able to walk into new situations with your dog knowing he is confident, flexible and able to adapt. Taking challenges and changes in stride is a vital skill you can help your puppy learn – and you'll both be glad you did.

Training a Shy Dog

It may be your instinct to comfort or reassure your dog or puppy when he acts shy, fearful or unsure; but that is reinforcing his fearful behavior. Remember, the approach to training is to ignore behavior that is unwanted and reward obedient behavior. If your dog is showing fear, hiding, cringing, or crying; to reassure him is equivalent to his pack leader showing approval – and you don't want to encourage fearful behavior.

As with other unwanted behavior, if your dog acts fearful or shy, just ignore the behavior. With time and experience, that behavior will shift as your dog encounters new situations, has a positive experience (in spite of his fear), and, as a result, gains confidence. That dynamic really doesn't need to involve you at all.

For example, perhaps you've seen your dog be uneasy at first with a new toy. He crouches and studies it; then he may make a practice lunge at it, to see if it lunges back. Next, he lunges and butts it with his head. He's experimenting; when nothing negative happens, he's likely to begin to play with the toy. There! He worked through his fear all on his own, and now has a bit more confidence and experience with new situations. When you're out, and your dog is fearful of something but willing to explore it, if it's safe, just let him. And keep yourself out of the experience; teach him he can work through his fear on his own, in his own way. When he has worked through it, and shows some confidence with the new person, animal or object, praise him.

Desensitizing Your Dog's Fear

When you work to desensitize your dog, you slowly introduce him to whatever he fears, in gradually more challenging ways. Start slow. Let's repeat that: start slow. Be patient.

In desensitization training for fear issues, your job is generally to put him in a new situation that is safe and let him work through things on his own. He may hide – let him. He may hold back and whine fearfully, or bark aggressively. Just be still. Secure him on collar and leash so you have some control, but don't respond to what he does. Give him all the time he needs to work past the fear and be at ease in the situation; forcing him to confront things he fears will only make him more fearful and possibly make him fearful of you, and you don't want that.

At the same time, do not ignore the aggressive fear-based behavior, such as biting, growling or snapping. You'll get a feel for what your dog is frightened of – cats, or strangers, or sirens, or someone carrying a broom or newspaper. When you know what triggers fear in your dog, introduce him to a situation that he fears slowly. And if he behaves aggressively, correct him. The best thing to do is to immediately reprimand him and correct him. Put him into a sit/stay. If he is out of control and remains out of control, you have moved ahead too quickly in your training. Remove him from the situation and desensitize him in less challenging ways until he has more confidence – then try exposing him to the safe, but fear-inducing element again.

If you correct him, put him in a sit/stay, and he obeys, immediately reward him. In this training, use big rewards – his favorite tidbit, and always, a great deal of praise. He has behaved in a way you want him to repeat; be sure he knows that.

Desensitizing Your Dog to Loud Noises

Some dogs are fully at ease with loud noises – fireworks, sirens, traffic, and thunder don't faze them. Other dogs become so fearful of loud noises that they become frenzied and panicked. Dog owners often report they have to deal with their dog's fear and negative reaction to such noises. Many dogs are so traumatized that all their training is ineffective and they are unable to function until the noise stops.

As always, any situation in which your dog is not in your control poses a danger to your dog and others. Your dog's fear may be apparent in his behavior – hiding under a table or bed (and possibly getting stuck there). Or he may destroy a sofa cushion, or defecate or urinate in the house. His responses are likely to be particularly extreme if he becomes afraid of loud noises when you are not at home; it's the reason many owners don't make plans to be out on holidays that involve fireworks. They stay home because they know their dog will be better able to cope if they do.

Your instinct may be to comfort and reassure your dog; don't. Again, to do so is to reinforce unwanted behavior. You are essentially rewarding him for being afraid. Think about it – you're giving him attention. He likes the sound of your voice; he likes to be petted – in giving him lots of attention, speaking to him and stroking him soothingly, you are telling him he's done the right thing in being afraid. No, no, no! Better to bring what you know about training and positive reinforcement of desired behaviors to this situation, to help your dog adjust.

As with other unwanted behavior, the best approach when your dog reacts to firecrackers, sirens or thunder is just to ignore him. You should, of course, behave responsibly – watch him to be sure he doesn't come to harm by running into furniture or becoming stuck under a table. But otherwise, stay out of the situation and let him work through things on his own.

Know your dog; know how he responds to noise. If you are going to be away, and your dog tends to hide under things when frightened by loud noises, be sure he can't get stuck under the bed while you're gone. You'll need to canvas your house for such threats and make sure you've addressed them before you leave the dog alone – not just during a time when you know there will be loud noises, but any time, since you never know when a siren or car backfiring might set your dog off.

Consider whether your dog would feel safer and more comfortable in a small room, or in his crate. It can be difficult to train your dog to deal with his fear of loud noises, but work with him until he can at least control his fears without destroying things, or hurting himself.

And when things are calm, and there are probably not going to be any unexpected noises, work with your dog using desensitization approaches. Get a recording of the sound of thunder, if he fears thunder. Play it back at a low volume when he's relaxed. Gradually increase the volume; ignore it if he responds negatively, but reward him for remaining calm.

This type of desensitization training can make a big difference in how your dog responds, but fear of noise is a very ingrained and strong fear in some dogs. Just the idea that they may have to deal with noise – as when you play sounds of thunder very softly – can make them panic. This fear isn't easy to cure, but with patience and hard work, you and your dog can better learn to cope with noises.

Using Distraction for Fearful Dogs

Distraction is a way to redirect your dog's attention away from what he fears, and toward something he feels more positive about. It takes his mind off his fear. For example, if it's a holiday and you know your dog fears the loud noises fireworks make, prepare in advance; gather his toys and some of his favorite treats so you can turn his attention elsewhere when the popping and explosions begin.

If your dog fears thunderstorm, you will need to be aware of his behavior – he will probably sense the onset of a storm before you do. When the skies are a bit dark and you see him beginning to act fearful and stressed, get out his toys and encourage him to play. He may be reluctant; still, try. Use treats, too, as a distraction. Or go with a combination – one of those toys that holds treats, encouraging the dog to roll and chase it, and to become absorbed trying to get the treat out.

Remember your goal to try to make challenging things pleasant; if a thunderstorm is imminent, or there are fireworks popping outside, play with your dog. He likely loves his time with you and will realize that the thing he fears also holds something positive for him. Those good associations can go a long way to replacing his fearful feelings.

Teaching Your Dog Not to Chew

Dogs chew. It's just a given. Every dog feels a need to bite, strengthen his biting muscles, and sharpen his teeth. You don't want to teach your dog not to chew at all; you want to provide him with things that he can chew and teach him only those things are to be chewed on. In doing so, you're affirming a good instinct, keeping him occupied and happy, and even helping him keep his teeth clean and plaque-free.

Problem chewing isn't just a matter of inconvenience; it's important to teach your dog what is and is not appropriate to chew for reasons of safety. If your dog chews through an extension cord, he can injure himself, and even cause a fire. If he ingests shards, you may be looking at a significant vet bill, or even risking that he'll eat something poisonous or harmful and die.

If chewing is still a problem even after giving your dog things he's allowed to chew, here are some ways to address inappropriate chewing.

When Your Puppy Chews Inappropriately

Siberian Husky puppies will chew on everything they can sink their teeth into. Just as you can expect your puppy to vocalize, chewing is just a given. And – just because it's normal doesn't mean you can't direct chewing to that your puppy learns to chew in ways that are acceptable and appropriate – his toys and rope pulls, rather than your shoes or the furniture.

Address unwanted chewing early on, before those little puppy teeth become the big, chomping teeth of a full-grown dog with a muscular jaw. Start by controlling the puppy's environment. Keep him in a small, puppy-proof room for the first few weeks, with toys to chew on, and away from things you don't want him chewing.

Give him a variety of chew toys, both to keep him from being bored (and thus feeling an even greater need to chew), and to give him appropriate items to chew. That way, your puppy will feel safe he can satisfy an instinctual need in a way that's acceptable.

Encourage him to play with his chew toys – praise him for playing with them, and in particular, for chewing them. That way he knows there are some things it's safe for him to chew. If he chews something he shouldn't, don't make a big deal about it. Remember – ignore behavior you don't want, unless it's dangerous behavior. Praise and reward behavior you do want. Take the item he shouldn't be chewing away from him, quickly, calmly and silently; offer him a toy, and when he takes it instead, praise him.

You can help your puppy understand it's good to chew his toys by capitalizing on his excitement when you first come home. As he enthusiastically runs to greet you, hand him one of his toys, and praise him when he takes it.

Keep your puppy's toys where he can easily get them, in a bowl or box that is only his, so he knows if it's an item in the bowl or box, it's OK for him to play with and chew. If you can, pick up and put away anything tempting that you don't want him chewing – throw rugs, for example, and very definitely put away your new leather boots. The things that carry your scent – your shoes, your hairbrush, even your used tissues – are particularly appealing to your puppy. Keep them out of his reach.

If the chewing continues, discourage your puppy by putting bad-tasting but non-toxic substances on items he chews, but shouldn't – Tabasco sauce, for example. The unpleasant reaction he has will help him choose the items you've provided that are appropriate for him to chew.

Conclusion

Training your puppy is not difficult – the guidelines are simple:

- Begin by earning your dog's trust and respect. You are his pack leader; if you can fulfill that role, his instincts will make training possible, and enjoyable for you both.

- Be consistent. You are teaching your dog what behavior you want, and what behavior you don't want. Your success depends on how clearly you convey appropriate behavior, and that requires that you respond consistently.

- Reward the behavior you want, and, unless it's dangerous behavior, ignore the behavior you don't want.

- Use your dog's instincts to your advantage.

- In addressing unwanted behavior, distract your dog from what you don't want him doing, and reward him for turning his focus elsewhere.

- Praise and reward consistently, generously and enthusiastically. Praise tells your dog what behavior you want. Moreover, it lets him know that good behavior is rewarded in ways he finds pleasant.

- Love your dog, by all means; but don't assume your dog's love for you means he also respects you. Respect comes from setting boundaries and clear expectations. Remember, the goal of training is to turn your dog's interest in doing what he wants, into complete willingness to do what you want.

- Address problem behavior. Problem dogs are a danger to you, to themselves, and to others. Train your dog early, and train correctly from the start. Put in whatever time and effort is needed to correct bad behavior.

- Be thoughtful of how training can best be accomplished. Keep training sessions short at first, when your dog's attention span is short. Give the training lots of time. Keep to a schedule for feeding, going to your dog's toilet area, and having play sessions and training sessions. Training is not difficult, but when done right, it is time-consuming; give it the time it needs to train your dog thoroughly and reliably.

- Bookend training with a fun period of play, to teach your dog training is a positive thing.

- Train in the proper order, starting with basic commands: heel, halt on command, sit on command, and sit/stay. When your dog well and truly masters these four commands, you've laid the groundwork for additional, more complicated commands.

And now — congratulations! You now know everything you'll probably need to know to train your dog well and thoroughly to be the companion animal you and your family will love and enjoy for years to come. If all goes well, you'll be training your dog in the more complex commands in just a matter of weeks.

Remember — always — to be patient and positive with your dog. Scaring your dog is abusive, and an abused dog develops behavior problems that are dangerous and difficult to correct.

By showing your dog patience and giving the training the time it needs to be done well, you're investing in a wonderful relationship that will reward you — and your dog — in the years to come.

Remember, there are no bad dogs; just poor trainers.

If you enjoyed learning about Siberian Huskies, I would be forever grateful if you could leave a review. Reviews are the best way to help authors and your fellow readers to find the good books so make sure to help them out!

Made in the USA
Columbia, SC
04 April 2023

14748647R00100